WILD DISCOVERY GUIDES

Ningaloo Reef - Shark Bay and Outback Pathways

Australia RRP $35:95
1st Edition 2005
2nd Edition 2012

GASCOYNE
DEVELOPMENT COMMISSION

Tourism is recognised as a growth industry in the Gascoyne region. The unique landscape and intriguing flora and fauna make the region a special place to visit. Through this guide book it is hoped that visitors to the Gascoyne can learn about and appreciate the natural beauty of the region and making the journey more memorable. The Gascoyne Development Commission was pleased to be able to support this project with the assistance provided through the Regional Development Scheme.

Len Zell
Susie Bedford

Front cover – A composite image of a whle shark, anemone and fish by Len Zell and dolphin feeding by Monkey Mia Wilsights Tours.

Back cover – a composite of images from the whole region – by Len Zell.

ISBN 978-0-9757184-5-2

Ningaloo Reef - Shark Bay coast and Outback Pathways region from space – a MODIS satellite image taken from first-ever cloud-free shot of the whole of Western Australia, August 2002. MODIS imagery provided by WASTAC digitally enhanced and produced by Satellite Remote Sensing Services, Department of Land Information, Perth, stern Australia. The page location of the maps used in the text are shown on this image.

PILBARA

Fortescue
River Basin

.Tom Price

. Newman

WESTERN AUSTRALIA

Page 148

Canning Stock Route

Yilgarn Plateau

. Meekatharra
Lake Anneen

. Wiluna
Lake Way

. Cue

Page 132

Lake Austin

. Sandstone

. Mt Magnet

Lake Noondie

Wild Discovery Guides™
Ningaloo Reef - Shark Bay and Outback Pathways
Len Zell[1]
Susie Bedford
[1]Adjunct Senior Lecturer School of Marine and Tropical Biology James Cook University Townsville Queensland 4811
Published by Wild Discovery Guides™
© Copyright Len Zell and Susie Bedford 2012
National Library of Australia Cataloguing-in-Publication entry

Author: Zell, Len.

Title: Wild Discovery Guides: Ningaloo Reef - Shark Bay and Outback Pathways / Len Zell, Susie Bedford; photographs by Len Zell.

Edition: 2nd ed.

ISBN: 9780975718452 (pbk.)

Notes: Includes bibliographical references and index.

Subjects: Shark Bay Region (W.A.)--Guidebooks. Shark Bay (W.A.)--Description and travel. Ningaloo Region (W.A.)--Description and travel. Ningaloo Region (W.A.)--Guidebooks. Murchison Region (W.A.)--Guidebooks Murchison Region (W.A.)--Description and travel. Gascoyne (W.A.)--Guidebooks. Gascoyne (W.A.)--Description and travel.

Other Authors/Contributors: Bedford, Susie.
Dewey Number: 919.413

Designed by Donna Stewart thevale_stewart@yahoo.com.au and Greg Nelson at Upside Creative
Photography by Len Zell unless otherwise acknowledged.
Set in 8.5pt Garamond

DISCLAIMER AND NOTES FOR THE READER

Although the authors and publisher have tried to make the information as accurate as possible, they accept no responsibility for any errors, omissions, loss, injury or inconvenience sustained by any person using this book. Whilst every care was taken in the research and production of this book it must not be used for any investment or real estate decision. Maps shown do not necessarily indicate a right of way and the information thus shown offers no warranty as to their accuracy whether supplied by the authors or a third party.

All things such as roads, management, custodianship and ownership of areas, facilities and the weather all change or we may have got them wrong. I accept full responsibility for this. I would appreciate knowing about any mistakes or errors for purposes of later correction. Please email me at len@lenzell.com so I can get it all right in the next edition - thanks.

Dedicated to:

by Len

my brothers Max, Jim, Frank and Neville and sister Enid who
have always said yes when I asked for help and for this
I love and thank them,

and

by Susie

To my brother Nick and sister-in-law Jenny for
all your support over the years.

Contents

The Authors

LEN ZELL

Adjunct Senior Lecturer, School of Marine and Tropical Biology, James Cook University.

Len's passion is the natural environment, especially coastal and coral reef systems. He has worked in research, management, ecotourism and education and around the world's reefs for more than 40 years.

He is particularly well known as the author of both editions of the Lonely Planet *Diving and Snorkeling - Great Barrier Reef*, both editions of *Wild Discovery Guides - Kimberley Coast, Wild Discovery Guides - Shark Bay-Ningaloo Coast and Outback Pathways* (with Susie Bedford), *Wild Discovery Guides – Australian Wildlife – ROADKILL, Wild Discovery Guides and Hema Maps – Great Australian Desert Tracks – Atlas and Guide* (with Ian Glover) and *Wild Discovery Guides – Flinders Island Tasmania*.

He has five other books in development. More information can be found on www.lenzell.com. He has appeared on many TV programs – as talent and researcher for the French Ushuaia group for their program on Australia with Nicolas Hulot (Len was their first and last Australian on the one hour shown in 2006), the award winning Channel 9 *Inside the Reef* series as field guide researcher and talent and has been on Channel 7 *11am*, ABC, Discovery, BBC and Fox.

Len has two species of coral named after him in recognition of his contributions to marine science during his employment at AIMS and GBRMPA. He also co-built and sailed a 13m yacht.

He has worked, dived, played and lectured throughout the world including the Great Barrier Reef, Kimberley Coast, PNG, French Polynesia, Cook Islands, Tonga, Easter Is, Pitcairns, Fiji, the Red Sea, Indonesia, Mediterranean and Caribbean.

He was chairman of Dive Queensland for two years and has served on the Council of the Australian College for Seniors. Len also worked on the wreck of the *Pandora* for six seasons with the Queensland Museum and was a director of the Pandora Foundation. He is a skilled lecturer, writer and underwater photographer/videographer. At the University of Queensland he established AustraLearn and TraveLearn. Len is also conducting research into sea level changes especially in relation to submerged caves and their human use and co-published a paper on the human constructions on Rankin Island in the Kimberley in June 2007. He has published many other papers and reports.

SUSIE BEDFORD

Susie is a science teacher who has been teaching for more than 25 years. In 2003 she was nominated for a "National Excellence in Teaching" award, and in 2006 won the Mid-west (Gascoyne) Education District's "Secondary Teacher of the Year", which made her a finalist in the Teacher of the Year award for WA. Before becoming a teacher she worked as a marine biologist, having completed both her B. Sc and M. Sc degrees at James Cook University, Townsville N.Qld.

She moved to Exmouth in 1997, after being compellingly spellbound by the area, when she and her son Ben spent 9 days camping, snorkelling and exploring Cape Range National Park and Ningaloo Reef. After gaining work as a diving instructor, she was then offered work teaching Science at Exmouth District High in July 1997 and she has been there ever since. Her passion for the marine environment and conservation saw her take on the Presidency of the Cape Conservation Group, a role she still holds many years later. She helped to set up the Ningaloo Community Turtle Monitoring Program, which uses volunteers to monitor beaches for nesting turtles during the nesting season. She still trains and assesses volunteers, and does monitoring when she gets a chance. She also instigated the group's "No plastic fantastic!" campaign aimed at reducing and eventually eliminating plastic bags from Exmouth and North West Cape.

In 2004 Susie was a state finalist in the WA Regional Achievers' Awards for her environmental and conservation work. Before moving to Exmouth she was the WA state president of the Marine Education Society of Australasia for 2 years. Aside from her passion for the environment, she likes to paint, play the piano, read, kayak, snorkel, dive, cycle and swim. An avid dog lover, her 2 crazy dogs help to keep her fit.

Preface

In this book we give you the option of taking several journeys – from the Ningaloo Coast World Heritage Area (including Cape Range National Park and) to the Shark Bay World Heritage Area, and their associated features. They are also identified and promoted as 'iconic Australian Landscapes' as promoted by Tourism Australia. Then for those wanting an outback adventure or two you can drive the Outback Pathways – the Wool Wagon Pathway, Kingsford Smith Mail Run or Miner's Pathway. This is a land of dramatically different landscapes from rich coral reefs, through seagrasses, muddy and sandy shores, mangroves, oysters on rocks and onto the arid lands of spinifex and rock strewn plains, limestone karst systems, dry river beds, the world's biggest monocline, salt encrusted pans and spectacular yellow and red sand dunes. We 'did' them all and loved every minute of it – the places we went and the people we met. Sadly we didn't have time to meet more and learn more ourselves!

Ningaloo Reef, Muiron Islands and Cape Range were recently incorporated into the Ningaloo Coast World Heritage Area (June 2011), while Shark Bay has been a World Heritage Area since 1991. Along with the Gascoyne-Murchison Outback Pathways, they are all within a day's drive northwards from Perth. These areas are seen in the satellite photo earlier in the book and for the purposes of general discussion we will refer only to the 'Region' here.

Ningaloo Reef to Shark Bay Coast extends along about 600 km of the coast and more than 1200km should you follow the coastline carefully. This is approximately from 21°40'S to 26°50'S. The Outback Pathways at 3000km in length are the longest series of self-drive trails in Australia and occur in the areas from between about 21°55'S to about 29°25'S and 113°40'E and 119°25'E.

Take the time to 'read the landscape' to help you understand the recent geological history of this coast. You can see the 'living fossils' or stromatolites at Hamelin Pool showing the earliest life forms on the planet (fossil forms are 3.5billion years old). Complex living organisms arrived later at about 350 million years ago. Here there have been great global changes progressing to the arrival of Aboriginal people more than 40 thousand years ago. Much of the evidence of their discovery and use of this coast is now under water due to rising sea levels. At the end of the last ice age – about 20,000 years ago – the waters rose and covered the continental shelf at an average rate of up to 1.3cm/year – was this The Great Flood? - ending about 5,000 years ago when sea level stabilised about 2m above present and down again to present levels then up 1.5m 3,000 years ago before dropping down again with a final jump up of 85cm and then down to the present level about 750 years ago.

The Aboriginal people had developed and lived an enormous amount of traditions, oral history and knowledge of the climate, land, flora and fauna. Much of this is yet to be interpreted in a way that uninitiated Aboriginals can understand. The information which non-Aboriginal people have been exposed to and/or caused to be lost indicates a history far richer and more valuable than any that is generally known and sadly it is poorly recorded. We have found that the more we learn about Aboriginal culture the more we value what it is and the more that we realise we should have learned much, much more from it.

An aspect of Aboriginal culture commonly used by non-Aboriginal people is the term 'Dreaming' to attempt to provide a meaningful description of the Aboriginal relationships to animals, plants, weather, seasons, the night sky, landforms and all aspects of their surrounds. We find the dreaming term far from adequate as their connections and relationship with so many places can only be described as deeply sacred, highly religious, core of the law and similarly strong terms indicating an enormous depth of this connection. As a consequence

Beautiful beaches to the north of Coral Bay show beach rock outcrops indicating older beach lines. LEN ZELL

Aboriginal paintings, petroglyphs, stone arrangements and many other works add to their use of this area as a deeply spiritual and core of their lives. LEN ZELL

Burringurrah has been an essential part of the neighbouring Aboriginal Language Groups for millennia. LEN ZELL

non-Aboriginal people tend to blunder through these stories or places of great Aboriginal significance with little or no understanding of their transgressions. Be aware of this wherever you are as we are always in 'their country'.

European recorded arrivals began in the 1600s with significant settlements occurring along this coast in the mid to late 1800s. With their arrival, up to 90% of the Aboriginals died of diseases, resources of the sea were overexploited, vegetation overgrazed, soils compacted and eroded and fauna displaced or sent to extinction. Feral animals continue to deplete native wildlife and weed species increase the displacement of native vegetation.

The present fauna and flora of the Cape Range (with its bizarre cave-dwellers), Ningaloo Reef, Shark Bay Coast and Outback Pathways are a great mixture of marine, coastal, semi-arid to arid and desert land communities. The almost benign geology with its resultant colours and soils determine the types of living organisms seen. This is a very special region because of the great diversity of habitats to be found. These provide a fabulous range of opportunities, from desert species through arid grasslands, woodlands, salt, mud, sand and seagrass flats, rocky platforms, blowholes, hypersaline pools and bays and mangroves over sea floors to coral reefs – some of the richest and most diverse habitats on the planet.

This book is an introductory guide only. We wish to *stimulate your imagination rather than satisfy your curiosity*. Visiting, you will constantly find places, information, plants and animals not covered by this book. Never fear as they may even be new to science or almost certainly will be mentioned in a guide specific to that group (which is in the reading list at the back of this book). This will also add to your sense of personal discovery.

This coast is under ever-increasing pressure from agriculture, recreational users, tour operations, commercial fishing, aquaculture and mining for iron ore, oil and gas. What were lands roamed by Aboriginal people and recently almost a wilderness experience is becoming more and more 'crowded'. More stringent management systems are necessary to protect these valuable cultural and natural resources and the processes that drive them so that they persist to be enjoyed by our descendants. This will also require greater expenditure on research, monitoring and education to ensure that we understand what cultural material, customs, natural processes and ecosystems there are and why they need careful treatment.

The Traditional Owners of the region are in the process of attempting to get back the rights to their country. The WA Department of Indigenous Affairs has legislation developing programs to protect cultural sites and the WA Department of Environment and Conservation (DEC - previously CALM) has put significant effort into this region to allow damaged sites to rehabilitate and control visitor access to, and use of, fragile areas. In addition, DEC and the CSIRO (in cooperation with the local communities), have developed several innovative animal breeding and protection programs to re-introduce species previously lost or badly depleted from the area. Aboriginal people are being used more and more in the management of and research into the local fauna and flora. Your appropriate behaviour at any sites visited will be appreciated by those who are responsible for them and those who follow.

Our success will be your closing of this book and going off to discover more – either in the library, on the web or best of all throughout this fabulous coast, its waters and along the Outback Pathways. We hope you enjoy the process and leave the areas in better shape, rather than degraded, as a result of your visit.

How to use this book

More than three hundred thousand tourists visit this region each year. Only a small fraction of them get to see any more than a superficial view of the area or to experience the outback regions. To stimulate their interests this book introduces the plants and animals with a photographic guide and captions. The primary habitats, climate, geology and 'icons' of the area are covered.

There is a satellite image for regional orientation and indication of the discrete area of study plus 11 maps covering the whole coast in sequence from north to south and the Outback Pathways. These maps are sections from Hema Maps taken from their Gascoyne and Murchison series. The legend for the maps is inside the back cover with the distance scale on each.

There are also "boxed bits" of information or hints associated with some aspect of each

LEN ZELL

Blue seastars stand out from amongst the coral – their colour is a powerful sunscreen.

LEN ZELL

Both pink and red versions of Sturt's Desert Pea occur in the region. The southern region has the highest number of wildflowers in Australia.

LEN ZELL

Bottlenose Dolphins randomly come to the beach at Monkey Mia to be fed occasionally by Rangers.

One of the many waterholes throughout the region.   LEN ZELL

section or allied subject in the text nearby, with some almost randomly placed. They are in a different text style and separated from the main text by colour or borders. Several of the safety notes are very important e.g. Dangerous Marine Animals, Driving Hints, Whale Watching guidelines, Cyclones and Fire. References to them are made in the Contents.

We then take you through the geology of the areas to provide the basis on which the major habitats, climate, human history and then plants and animals exist. To ensure a comprehensive experience we have provided a trip through each of the areas to give coherence to the information herein. Again we emphasise that this book is introductory and we strongly encourage you to always look well beyond what we and others provide as background for your travels. There will always be something happening in front of you that no-one else has ever seen– if you don't look you won't see!

To complement the book are a reading list and index, at the back, to both expand your experience should you want and also to speed access to what is in this book. The Chapter of Important Contacts covers web sites, management agencies, local governments, community groups and others that will enhance your knowledge, understanding of and access to the areas.

For those driving NORTH to SOUTH or SOUTH to NORTH we have put an asterisk at the beginning of each block of information so those travelling in the opposite direction to the text can use these points to read the journey backwards.

Use of scientific and common names

All scientific names are shown in italics, eg *Tursiops truncatus* for Bottlenose Dolphins or *Rhincodon typus* for the Whale Shark. Thus a common name will have capitals when the actual species discussed can be identified as shown with Bottlenose Dolphins or Whale Sharks. If all dolphins or more than one species is used there will be no capitals as in 'dolphins or sharks'. In the main we have avoided the use of scientific names as they are available in the specific guides for each group.

Naming of features

Wherever the origin of a place name is included it will be shown as e.g. Carnarvon (British Secretary of State in 1883 – Lord Carnarvon). The Aboriginal people had names for all the areas in this text and under international convention these names should have priority. Sadly we did not have the resources to find all these.

Acknowledgements

We are highly indebted to the many people who encouraged and helped us during the production of this book – thanks to all of you. The biggest thank you to Donna Stewart and Greg Nelson who designed the book – their patience and skills took the basic raw materials and produced a product to be very proud of – again! Dan Byrnes Word Factory's editing added significantly to the final product. We would also like to thank Hal Payne, Coralie and Neil McLeod, Matt Sharpe, Paul and Liz Wittwer, Stephen Boyd and Neil Hayward for their support. We thank the Gascoyne Development Commission for their assistance through funding and guidance which allowed us to include the outstanding Outback Pathways. The WA Department of Environment and Conservation (DEC) staff continues to do a great job in difficult circumstances. Thanks to Anne Preest and Elders, the late Sid Dale and Maureen Dodd of the Gnulli people. Local Governments and their Information Centres and Libraries were of substantial help and we gratefully thank them and their staff. We also acknowledge the use of all the texts in the Reading List at the back of this book. Their insights, thoughts, photographs, maps, diagrams and information helped us better understand the Ningaloo Reef, Shark Bay and Outback Pathways. We accept full responsibility for our interpretations of their information should we be inaccurate or in disagreement with them I accept full responsibility for that. Phil Dodd's web research, field assistance and photography were especially helpful. Paul and Pam Dickenson at Steep Point who were rangers for the area. Thanks to those photographers who are acknowledged on each of their photos. Without their images this book would be incomplete. They include Madeleine Zell, Phil Dodd and Harvey Raven.

Thanks to those unsung heroes who helped us by the roadside, told us where to go, repaired tyres and otherwise made our journey successful. Telstra's Mobilesat telephone system ensured we had great communications wherever we went – truly "No worries" - a great boon to our safety and capacity to do a better job.

Western Australia has a wonderful asset in their very helpful and professional staff of the Department of Land Information who allowed the reproduction of parts of their wonderful WASTAC MODIS satellite image. We also thank Hema Maps for their professionalism and supply of their maps. And to those wonderful people of the region and those we have missed here – THANK YOU.

Ningaloo Reef – Shark Bay and Outback Pathways – a general introduction

Spinifex clumps create microenvironments amongst small shrubs. Cape Range coast.

LEN ZELL

This book covers from just south of the Shark Bay World Heritage Area about 800km north of Perth north up the coast to include Ningaloo Coast World Heritage Area, which includes Ningaloo Reef, Cape Range and the Muiron Islands, then east to include Exmouth Gulf and the mangroves on its eastern side. We then go inland onto the three longest self-guided trails in Australia – The Outback Pathways. The region is bordered to the north by the Pilbara - another book!

The Ningaloo Coast World Heritage Area offers an opportunity to see rich living coral reef systems and those that are dead 'time capsules' which were thriving reefs when sea level was 5m higher 125,000 years ago. These can now be seen on the western edge of Cape Range as dry terraces. Ningaloo Reef is a new layer of coral reef over a fossil coral system that was last fully covered more than 60,000 years ago. Add to this the 30 million year old sea floor of Cape Range that is now a range folded up and out of the water, and dissolved by acidic rainwater producing a limestone karst system incorporating masses of caves, caverns, underground water reservoirs with strange life forms and you start to get a picture of why this area is so special. Swimming, diving, snorkelling, boating, walking, caving, fishing or just lying around and enjoying are all excellent ways to experience this area. Or for a real buzz jump in a plane to see it from the air to better understand it.

This is a rugged and vast landscape – a timeless land that was the home of Aboriginal people for thousands of years until the guns, germs and steel of the Europeans killed them off or displaced them.

Many known shipwrecks dating back to the 1600s, pearling industry dramas, wartime traumas, agricultural successes and failures and vibrant local communities overlay thousands of years of Aboriginal occupation of these lands and sea floor above 130m depth. There is possible evidence that the Chinese visited this coast in the 1420s and possibly others several thousand years earlier. Rich life occupies the great diversity of unique habitats with several areas of world significance. Dugong herds, rich seagrass meadows, Aboriginal sites and disease lockup islands, fishing industry, tourism facilities, mining and agriculture within an historical framework offer many opportunities for those wishing to take the time to look and observe.

Shark Bay provides a Mecca for the scientist, archaeologist, boaties, fishers, tourists and students. Sandy peninsulas, shallow bays and stark landscapes offer more challenges than most of us wish to accept. Those of the more gentle life can still see most of what the region has to offer with tour operators and by wandering along the accessible roads and waterways. Aerial opportunities also allow excellent perspectives of what the region has on offer just not understandable by other means.

Outback Pathways

These three self-drive pathways are the longest in Australia and give you an exposure to the true 'outback'. The rolling plateau to the west has provided a mining and grazing bonanza for the Europeans who arrived here in force in the mid to late 1800s. The ancient geology has quite a different form to the plains off the plateau between it and the coast both of which are also important grazing lands. These arid alluvial plains, which are the washed off remnants of the plateau, lead into the sand dune covered coastal plains. The dune belts when seen mapped, provide an image of swirling lines all indicating different wind directions and strengths when they were formed about 25,000 years ago when Australia was dry during the last glaciation or ice-age event.

This recent European history is full of tales of woe to success – dreams, deaths, hardships, political shenanigans, exploitation, transport methods and routes - all providing a colourful

From the western-most point of the Australian continent it is possible to see the uplifted layers of Tamala Limestones that are the basis of all the neighbouring country.

LEN ZEL

backdrop and canvas on which you can paint your own pictures. The use of the law, not always in a lawful manner, to control and remove people is a disturbing history for those who delve into it.

The European name of the region – the Gascoyne Murchison - is taken from the two primary rivers that drain it. As rivers they are little more than a string of waterholes most of the year waiting for the rainy periods. The Gascoyne River (Sir George Grey after a military friend in 1839) which drains an area of almost 7 million hectares extending about 500 kilometres inland, is the largest, with the Lyons River (Mithering to the Aboriginal people – after Admiral Lyons by Gregory in 1858) feeding into it. All the rivers flow occasionally between February and August. They also re-charge the underground aquifers which feed into the ocean from under the sand. Some of these aquifers are the primary water supply of coastal settlements. The Murchison River (Grey - after Sir Frederick Murchison, president of the Royal Geographical Society) drains an area of just over 82,000 km2 extending about 550 km inland onto the Yilgarn Plateau.

The Kennedy Ranges (Gregory after WA Governor) and Burringurrah (Mt Augustus), the world's largest monocline, stand proudly above the plateau, each with totally different geology and Aboriginal mythology. They are fabulous places to delve into the Aboriginal history of the land and need more time than indicated for doing the drive. Take at least an extra one to two days for each.

As you drive these pathways you will discover brochures available at information centres as well as interpretive signs and parking areas at each of the special points of interest. We have covered each of these in this book to complement your experience.

There are numerous such pools in the river courses throughout the region and as Frank Wittenoon (2003) said these pools were surrounded and filled with Aborigines trying to keep cool as they dies from influenza and whooping cough and other European carried diseases.

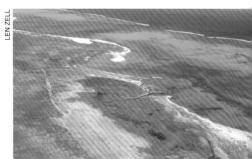

Two of the most important marine systems beside each other – a coral reef and a mangrove community – both highly susceptible to small changes in temperature, sediments and especially oil.

The Queen of the Murchison in Cue. One of the many grand establishments built on the gold flowing from the area. It is now the scene of an annual gathering of queens of a different type!

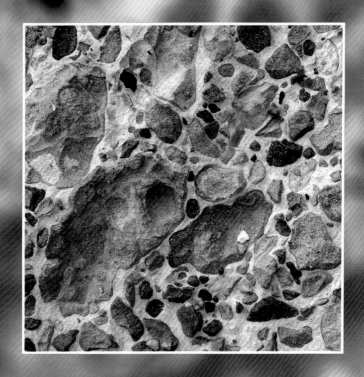

Geology and Geomorphology

Multicoloured rocks in limestone, Steep Point.

The coastal and land features of this area overlay the original rocks and magma formed at or near Earth's beginning about 4.6 billion years ago. Those features we can study are all less than 600 million years of age – all times that challenge one's capacity for numbers! Western Australia is a stunning and dramatic display of rocks and processes, from truly ancient to recent, not to be seen elsewhere. Keep in mind that over the billions of years, great chunks of the Earth's crust joined together and broke up forming seas, continents, mountains and all the time floating around on different parts of the Earth's surface. These tectonic plate movements caused periods of ice ages, mountain growth and erosions and massive volcanic eruptions, lava flows and intrusions below the surface cooling and forming more rocks. In addition Earth has been through 'ice-house periods' each of about 75 million years interspersed with 'hot house periods' each of about 200 million years. (Johnson, 2009) It was during these hot house periods that animals and plants flourished and were then buried forming the coal, oil and gas reserves we tap today.

The vivid red of the iron attached to the sand grains provides the colour in the dunes of Francois Peron National Park – here at Cape Peron.

Today this region has immense alluvial plains and red dunal systems in between the low remnant sedimentary ranges – the Kennedy and Collier Ranges, wide alluvial valleys due to the drainage patterns developed by the river flows of the Gascoyne, Murchison, Lyons, Minilya, Lyndon and Ashburton Rivers.

The Australian continent is made up of several primary pieces – the eastern cratons (big pieces of continental landmasses floating on the Earth's surface) and then the Kimberley and Pilbara cratons that joined up a couple of billion years ago. It has been down and back to the South Pole at least once!

Over 430 million years ago (ma) Western Australia was uplifted. This led to the development of riverine sedimentary deposits in the Shark Bay area with deltaic river mouth deposits to the north until we reach Cape Range where it remained a shallow sea – the beginnings of the Carnarvon Basin. This persisted to about 405ma and then the sea receded until 387ma when the sea encroached over the coast from about Carnarvon to Onslow. This continued with some marine deposition until 300ma when this whole coast was submerged again with more sea floor sedimentation occurring.

Over the last 60 million years the area continued drifting north from the South Pole, at about 8cm/year, and continues to do so. India and Antarctica peeled away from what became the Western Australian coastline. As the area was inundated by the sea, this allowed sediments to wash down from the higher land masses and deposition of marine sediments some 200m thick.

Receding seas 245ma exposed the area from Shark Bay to Coral Bay again. Coastal and marine sedimentation then occurred from Coral Bay north until about 190ma when this area exposed again only to be resubmerged 175ma and then re-emerging 145ma for about 20 million years.

Gold surveys continue to yield growth of the gold industry again.   LEN ZELL

The old mines, and this, the brewery in the breakaway, show us the rock strata that make this such a stunning area not to mention the human history that could tell many a tale!   LEN ZELL

The western area of this book, the Gascoyne Sub-basin, lies within the Carnarvon Basin, a large sedimentary basin, almost entirely marine in origin, lying along and sloping gently towards the WA coast. It is characterised by low hills, open riverine flats and large rolling plains of sand. Sediments are about 4.5km thick with the oldest not being exposed to the south. There are some exposures of Precambrian rocks over 590 million years old (myo) that cause a higher series of hills and valleys with clearer drainage patterns. To the east of this area is the Yilgarn Plateau with its oldest rocks also being more that 600 myo – the gold country!

This all left us with several primary landform types, the erosional systems in the east, depositional in the central and coastal margins to the west. If you get to look at a map showing heights of the region these distinct zones become obvious with the plateau above 375m, central plain from 70-250m and the coastal margin from below 50m to sea level. Two well known exceptions inland are the Kennedy Ranges and Mt Augustus (Burringurrah) standing well above the general landscape and to the west the Cape, Rough and Giralia Ranges are all above the coastal plains. Throughout the central plain and coastal margin there are extensive windblown dune systems and many smaller range systems.

The north eastern areas of the region in the Bangemall Basin are covered with 1,600 myo sediments of shale, sandstone and dolomite. Some low grade metamorphism has occurred with folding and intrusion by sills of dolerite in many places. The rocks tend to be very heavily weathered or covered by soil and/or wind-blown sands.

The Bullara Sunklands run from Exmouth Gulf to Shark Bay and this low lying area includes Lake MacLeod – all formed as sea level dropped a few metres in the last 5,000 years.

Offshore the continental shelf overlies the western section of the Canning Basin which like many other continental shelves of erosional origins, overly coal, oil and gas reserves.

Shark Bay Geology

During the 1950s the first geological research into Shark Bay was instrumental in letting the world know of this amazing place with the publicising of the living fossils - stromatolites. Shark Bay is presently a shallow double bay, enclosed by the mainland, seawards by the Edel Land Peninsula, Dirk Hartog, Dorre and Bernier Islands. These islands and peninsulas are old north-south dune systems, from wind-blown calcareous sands over the last million years, sitting on top of old limestone systems and showing evidence of three sea level rises or transgressions. Underneath them has been folding, creating ridges which we see now as the peninsulas and islands extending out from them. The Peron Peninsula has a similar structure to the western peninsulas and it divides Shark Bay into two. It consists of wind-blown red sands, forming long parallel dunes interconnected by smaller dunes with land-locked salt or gypsum-rich lakes or birridas (See boxed bit on page 22) – the Aboriginal term for these playa lakes. The lakes are usually dry and are rich in gypsum, some of which has been mined in the past.

A line of cliffs, known as the Zuytdorp Cliffs, up to 270m high south of the areas covered by this dune system, runs 200km south from Dirk Hartog Island and Steep Point to Kalbarri. The cliffs were formed by a fault in the Tamala Limestone and it has probably been relatively stable for at least 2 million years.

The exposed limestones along the Zuytdorp Cliffs tell a tale to those who can read it.

Aerial views of Cape Range allow one to see its heavily dissected landscape, valleys, sinkholes and more.

The Tamala Limestone (1.8myo), up to 300m thick with about five different layers, formed from wind-blown calcareous sands and sandstones during a dry low sea level period with extremely strong southerly winds. They also exhibit sections that were formed whilst they were underwater. The exposures of these rocks can be seen from Dirk Hartog Island southwards for over 200km. Parts of the Zuytdorp (pronounced Zirtoff) Cliffs named after the *Zuytdorp* wrecked 60km south of Shark Bay in 1712 –have fossils of old corals exposed.

This spectacular section of the coast extends south to Kalbarri. By standing on the cliff tops it is possible to see the different layering of old rocks and how they erode at different rates forming ledges caves and blow holes. The Tamala Limestone can also be best experienced close up along the tops of these cliffs where the sharp weathered limestone surfaces are swept clean by the winds and dissolved by the slightly acidic rainwater. The sand dunes of Edel Land are up to 60m high and now are quite stable and overlay the older limestone below.

Big and Little Lagoons are birridas, both with a connection to the sea, and as such provide very important breeding or nursery areas for many species of fish and other marine

Birridas

LEN ZELL

The term birrida is a local Aboriginal name. Best seen on the Peron Peninsula where more than 100 of these round, oval or elongate depressions occur, from tens of metres to several kilometres long where they run between sand dune ridges. They were first formed over 20,000 years ago as the result of evaporating water, leaving behind gypsum that was picked up as it ran across or through the sand.

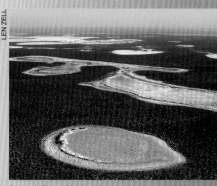

Francois Peron Natonal Park has many birridas – here with Big Lagoon in the background.

An interesting feature often seen in the birridas is an uplifted central area almost a metre higher than a moat that rings around its outside. This has been caused by the old gypsum, deposited more than 10,000 years ago being dissolved by recent groundwater. Careful observers will see small domes, forming on the surface of the moat floors, where the salt crystals under the surface form as the water dries and pushes the crust upwards. The groundwater can also rise with periods of high tides in the region and fill some moats. During wet periods and especially after rain many small planktonic animals can be seen in the water providing a feast for wading birds. These animals are mostly brine shrimp and other invertebrates that lie dormant as encapsulated eggs until the water arrives and then masses hatch to start their cycle again.

life. Salt resistant plants grow on the uplifted centres of the birridas and other species such as sandalwood, a few grasses and saltbushes can sometimes be found there, almost always around the outside.

These are very fragile systems and any tracks made in them will remain for many years. So, if driving through a birrida on a track, then please stay on the track as it is very easy to bog and the salt is not good for the car's metal! The thin salt crust has caught many an unwary walker or driver.

While "reading the Shark Bay landscape" today it is important to remember that all the systems you see were formed or modified during the glacial or interglacial periods over millions of years, with the last few hundred thousand years providing most of what we see now. You can see 145 (myo) chalks - in the east of the area exposed as calcretes with mudstones and some chert nodules. The red wind-blown sandstones, from 5-65 myo, and resultant moving dunes, are best seen on the Peron Peninsula extending to the south and on Faure Island. The western side of the Peron Peninsula is part of the Tamala Limestone overlying the sandstone below. There are several marine and terrestrial limestones, rocks formed from evaporation of shallow seas and then recent sands, beach ridges and both fossil and growing stromatolites (See boxed bit on page 23).

On the west side of Hamelin Pool it is possible to see circular 'blue holes' from the air. These were caused by the collapse of caves formed during the last ice age, a dry period, as rainwater washed down through the earth. Today they are filled with very salty water. Less salty incoming tidal waters sit on top of the deeper, very blue water which becomes extremely hot (to 50°C) but as the waters mix they become greenish and cooler.

The northern boundary of Hamelin Pool is a sand ridge, covered in seagrasses, the Faure Sill, formed from about 4,200 years ago, and this has prevented the present sea fully flushing Hamelin Pool see below. This, along with a maximum tidal range of about 1.6m (40cm daily average range), high temperatures, low rainfall and resultant high evaporation rates caused it to become hypersaline, thus lacking in grazing and competing marine organisms. This is ideal for the growth of stromatolites that we can see at Hamelin Pool (see boxed bit). Its salinity is almost double that of normal sea water. The biggest water movement here was during a cyclone when it rose 4m showing how atmospheric pressure can have dramatic effects on enclosed waters.

Bivalve (twin shelled) molluscs which thrive in hypersaline waters formed the Hamelin Pool and Lharidon Bight beach ridges and are mined in a small way today. Fortunately vehicles are now prohibited from the Shell Beach area so that we can see an area in rehabilitation, and walk on this amazing legacy of so many small animals.

Concretion of the shells into a soft rock occurs from percolating rainwater water carrying dissolved limestone which precipitates out and cements the shells together. As such it is suitable for use as a building material as can be seen in Denham and at the Hamelin Pool

Stromatolites
(means layered rocks)

LEN ZELL

Recently discovered in 1954, stromatolites are growing domes of usually laminated cyanobacteria and blue-green bacteria. When they were discovered it created a scientific sensation as they were previously only known as fossils. These were the first life forms on Earth as old as 3.5billion years and remain as the simplest single-celled life form today. Since 1954 other examples of stromatolites have been found in Western Australia and elsewhere in the world.

These ancient formations, once only known as fossils, have nine different living forms in Shark Bay Hamelin Pool. These intertidal forms lead out to those always submerged several metres in height.

It was the oxygen produced by these primitive organisms which reached a level sufficient for oxygen dependent animals to evolve about 1000 mya and it also allowed the deposition of iron (2 billion years ago) from the water – we see these massive iron deposits in other parts of WA today. Initially, as the iron was being deposited oxygen was only about 1% of the atmosphere, however when all the iron was deposited the oxygen gradually increased to the present day level of 21%. On a hot still day you may see the bubbles of oxygen being produced and streaming to the surface.

The Hamelin Pool water is so salty it stops grazing snails from eating the micro-

This form of stromatolite is permanently submerged and has quite a different layering of life on its surface, grows at a different rate and is still highly susceptible to touch.

LEN ZELL

organisms that grow the domes and also stops the growth of seaweeds and algae which would out-compete them. This plus the ready availability of calcium carbonate in the water allows the stromatolites to successfully occupy this niche. They were once common in ancient times but the arrival of the grazing and burrowing animals destroyed them and shading plants out-competed them. In essence a trip to Hamelin Pool waters is a trip back to at least early Palaeozoic times of more than 500mya. The living stromatolites you see today are only about 3000 years old.

Stromatolites can form reefs which protect the beaches and may form lines following the directions of the wave action. They also occur as dead rows above the high tide line, formed when sea levels were 1-2m higher, and continue in various forms to 4m below the surface. Moving sands have killed some only to be covered again with cyanobacteria when the sand was shifted off. There are many easily seen dead examples – some are red possibly from iron staining or bacterial effects. Others killed by the moving sands stay dead when re-exposed and we don't know why.

The varying combination of the living elements cause nine different living mat types and from these three primary growth forms develop – *pustular mats* form spongy mats over the substrate and sometimes column and mound shaped stromatolites in the higher intertidal, *smooth mats* are the slowest growing and build smaller columns and mounds in the lower intertidal and the *colloform mats* grow the fastest at up to 0.5mm/year and build sub-tidal columns and mounds. Because of the relatively stable salinity and constant immersion these also have a greater range of life associated with and on them. Usually about a centimetre below the surface of each column or dome the stromatolites begin to turn into rock – how this occurs is still unknown. Substrates will also have a major effect on the type found, with the columns and domes forming on rocky substrates and only mats on sandy bay beaches.

Please don't touch the stromatolites as doing so will kill these extremely slow growing communities. If you did, you would feel the sticky surface that catches sediments and slowly turns to rock. Scientists are still studying how these layers reflect the climates, day lengths and other changes that occurred as they grew hundreds and even millions of years ago and thus get clues to life on Earth then.

In addition to the organic growth, more occurs from the collection of sediments by a sticky film on the surface of each cell, with some carbonate deposition from chemical processes. Because of their incredibly slow growth rates, erosion during a storm can wipe out many years of growth. Normal daily water movement in the intertidal ensures an almost static size to the stromatolites here. Wagon tracks made over 70 years ago still look as fresh as when they were made, indicating the fragility and need for management of these sites, as any damage will be seen for many centuries.

Interpretive site. Progression from loose shells to the soft rock occurs as you move landwards from the sea into the oldest deposits which are about 4,000 years old and about 10m thick.

Cape Range Geology

20-30 million years ago the Cape Range area was a sea floor covered in fine sediments with dead plant and animal remains floating down. These consolidated into limestone rock over 10kms thick and older the deeper you go. About 15 million years ago the movements of the Australian plate caused the area to be forced into folds and the Cape, Rough and Giralia

Yardie Creek is another sliced view of the
Cape Range geology.   LEN ZELL

Terraces seen along the western side of
Cape Range indicate uplift of the Cape and
differing sea levels with coral growth.   LEN ZELL

As you fly into Learmonth you are able to
see the changing colours and directions of
the dunes at the head of the Gulf.   LEN ZELL

Ranges were pushed up as anticlinal folds bringing the sedimentary sea floor rocks to the top of the ranges we see today. It is probable that uplift is still occurring. Recent periods of sea level changes due to ice ages and continuing uplift of the range has meant that we see old coastal features like reef and wave cut terraces from 6 to 60m above sea level, with reef 120,000yo formed sediments forming a coralline bench 1-2km wide and 5-10m thick on the plain - all dry today.

The western range has four distinct terraces cut into the limestone from high sea stands during the last 500,000 years as well as canyons, creeks and alluvial fans from erosion - all developing at different times. The coastal plain was last underwater about 40,000 years ago and the sediments we see today were laid down up until this time. They are very similar to these we see offshore today. Some areas of the plain are covered with older material washed down from the range and appear as smooth rocks and pebbles - forming extensive alluvial fans often extending into the sea and seen as rounded stones in creeks and on some beaches. Sand dunes have formed along the shore where some are mobile but others vegetated and stable. They have originated from the breakdown of reef corals, mollusc shells and algae offshore - all showing the dynamic nature of these systems. The enormous teeth of the ancient *Megalodon* shark have been found in the area allowing some reasonable dating of those sediments.

The canyon structures we see today often follow fault lines in the range with smaller features like sink holes and cave or cavern systems following smaller cracks and sometimes tree root holes. This is known as a karst system, which describes a landscape formed by dissolution (not erosion) of rocks, particularly limestone.

As the range was uplifted and the caves and karst systems formed, it became increasingly porous and as the sea levels rose to their present height, the freshwater gradually ponded to form a freshwater lens/aquifer on top of the heavier salt water inside the range and plain - similar to those formed on coral cays or sand islands. The porosity of the range means that any pollutants or sediments, developed by humans and discharged into the system will percolate down impacting the fauna in these underground aquifers. Authorities need to carefully monitor the pumping of water from the freshwater lens to ensure it is not replaced with salty or brackish water.

There are two local dune systems – at the tip of the Cape and in the plains abutting the south of Exmouth Gulf. The dunes are formed of red siliceous sands, blown in from outside the area in both locations - those to the south have more marine carbonates giving them a camel colour. Older sand dunes are now the basis of some islands in the southern Exmouth Gulf partially immersed under a rising and now relatively stable sea. Note that some of the coastal dunes have an interesting history, as they were over-washed by tsunamis and storm surges during cyclones thus confusing those trying to determine their history today.

Coastal Geomorphology - Ningaloo Reef, Cape Range and Shark Bay

During the last 400,000 years this whole coast has been underwater and dry again four times. The last ice age finished about 18,000 years ago, with the sea rising from 130m below present to 2m above about 5,300 years ago. It dropped again to present levels and then rose back up to 1.7m above the present about 3,400 years ago, down and up again to 0.7m above present about 700 years ago. Note that this means that there was a period of 10,000 years where the sea rose at an average of 1.3cm per year as the ice caps melted. People are presently stressing about a few centimetres rise in the last 50 years!

Ningaloo Reef

Ningaloo Reef is the world's longest fringing reef, 'protecting' the coast from the strength of the ocean and providing a spectacular experience for those who place their heads underwater. The reef runs into the shore in places and is separated by a shallow lagoon in most areas. Passages eroded through the reef allow good boating access to diving and fishing locations on the outer reef, where the bottom drops away to about 30m close in. The reef extends more than 300kms from North West Cape to Red Bluff north of Carnarvon.

Various small reef formations, including kidney coral bommies are found in Exmouth Gulf which is bounded by beaches and mangroves along its western shores, tidal flats and mangroves to the south and then tidal flats, bays and inlets on its eastern margin, which boasts a regionally significant coast of arid zone mangroves and ancient algal mats. The top of the reef as we see it today was re-immersed only about 8,000 years ago and is a new layer of coral growth formed over that which had been exposed during beginnings of the last ice-age from about 60,000 years ago.

Shark Bay

The present-form Shark Bay is a recent occurrence, with new sand dunes overlying old limestone and sandstone running northwest, dividing the bay. The dunal structures seen today resulted from sea level changes in the last 20,000 years. As the sea moved up and down, the sand formed by erosion of the underlying rocks, and from coral and algal growth offshore, was pushed into the dunes. The Bullara Sunklands are an old coastal underwater plain that has been exposed in the last few thousand years. We see this in Shark Bay and Lake MacLeod to the north ending in Exmouth Gulf where you can see the sloping base extend into the southern gulf.

The Wooramel Seagrass Bank of more than 10,000 hectares extends 130km along the eastern shore of Shark Bay and is one of the largest limestone deposits formed by plants and animals in a modern environment.

A complex of limestone rocks, which runs from south of Shark Bay to the tip of Dirk Hartog Island and along the western margin, has formed into a long series of cliffs due to a fault in the Earth's crust. These cliffs reach 220m high, well south and 170m adjacent to Shark Bay. The limestone complex continues to the north with less spectacular cliffs

Sea urchins graze the reef for any detritus or other organic foods and may attach other items to themselves to aid in camouflage.

INSET The constant wave action of the Indian Ocean washes ground up corals and shells up and down these channels, up onto the reef top and over into the lagoon, often to be washed out through passes in the reef.

LEN ZELL

with blowholes and spectacular coastline well past Point Cuvier. These cliffs and coastal limestone exposures are backed by old beach ridges and coastal sand dunes often with salt pans behind. This coast is open to the full force of the Indian Ocean causing spectacular seas, blow holes and rogue waves that suck people off the rocks, generally to their death.

Inland Geomorphology

Over the recent millennia the coastal and inland plains developed during periods of wetter climate and changing sea levels. The erosion of the inland Yilgarn Plateau formed wide alluvial valleys to its west. Sediments were carried down by the Gascoyne, Lyons, Murchison, Wooramel, Minilya, Lyndon and Ashburton Rivers into their drainage basins and then to the sea. The wide alluvial plains have many red

The Shark Bay seagrass beds can be seen from space.

dune belts running in the directions of the old wind systems that made them.

The sedimentary Kennedy Ranges have been eroded into a spectacular feature that is now a National Park. The range covers 172,000ha and extends for 195 kilometres with incised canyons on the eastern side and springs on the west as the water from within the range makes its way out. Fossils and gemstones are found in the area. On top of the range are a series of red sand dunes showing that the sand for the dunes is sourced locally. The dunes on the sides of the road entering the park are almost identical.

Burringurrah or Mount Augustus is the world's largest rock rising to 858m - a granite intrusion under sedimentary rocks. Careful examination will show the monoclinal fold and where the nearby land has been eroded away.

Over the last century and a half, the grazing effects of vegetation removal and soil compaction have caused massive erosion of the soils of the whole region. Agricultural practices are improving so as to reduce this, but the evidence of this overgrazing can still be seen. Desertification can result and there is argument at the moment, as to whether the situation has reached an irreversible point leading to a drying of the whole area.

Sloping sandstone strata give some indication of the sedimentary origins of the Kennedy ranges.

Climate

Pools after rain dry quickly. Carnarvon - Mullewa Road.

The best time to visit this whole region is between March and October/November although more and more people are finding anytime is OK as long as they are well prepared for the heat and occasional cyclone!

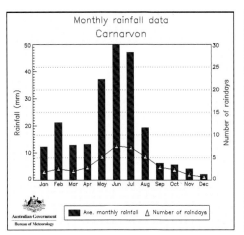

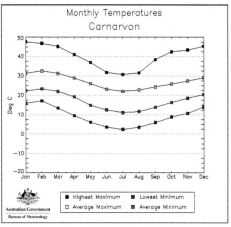

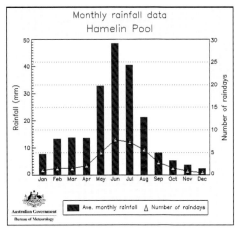

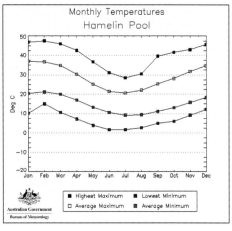

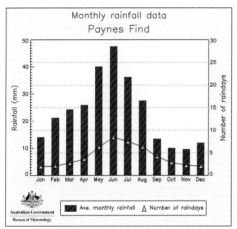

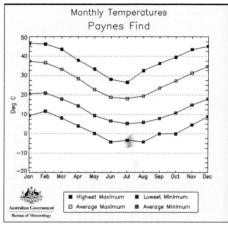

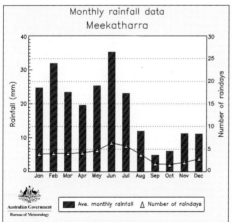

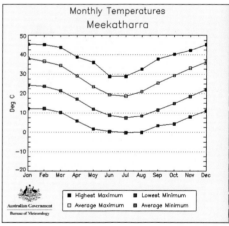

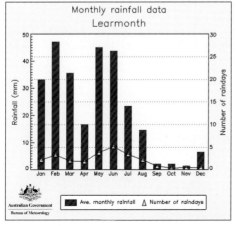

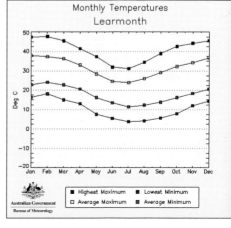

Average Annual
Minimum Temperature

Degrees
Celsius

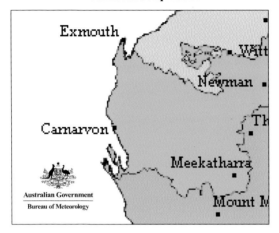

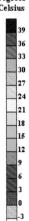

Average Annual
Maximum Temperature

Degrees
Celsius

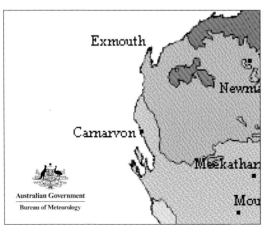

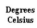

Cyclones

When a wind rotating in a circular motion reaches speeds of more than gale force (63km/h) it is classed as a cyclone and given a name. Cyclones are associated with low atmospheric pressure as hot air rises from a heating sea's surface sucking air into the centre creating a spiralling area of vertically rising air with a still centre called an eye. The whole cyclone can be hundreds of kilometres across reaching wind speeds of more than 220km/hr near the eye with speeds decreasing the further you move away from the centre. The eye of the cyclone is an eerily still place after the winds pass over with reverse winds hitting soon after as the whole system moves across the Earth's surface at speeds up to 100km/hr. It is the combination of the circular motion with the speed of the whole cyclone over the land that gives the maximum wind speeds. Learmonth Meteorological Office recorded Australia's fastest wind speed of 267km/hr during cyclone Vance! There have been faster wind speeds but the anemometers broke before the maximum was reached!

The Bureau of Meteorology's website www.bom.gov.au has excellent information on all aspects, as well as hourly updates on cyclones and all weather. Cyclones are graded into categories from 1-5 according to wind strengths with 1 being winds to 90km/hr and 5 being greater than 200km/hr and highly destructive. Once over land the cyclones tend to die and develop into rain depressions bringing massive rainfalls and associated floods.

Local radio stations broadcast regular updates and all local authorities have guides as to what you should do during a cyclone alert. The alerts are given colour codes with BLUE meaning a cyclone has formed and you need to start preparing for a cyclone, YELLOW means the cyclone is moving closer and you need to take action and RED you need to take shelter immediately.

The tropical arid conditions found along this coast are an interesting mix of influences brought about by the monsoonal tropical conditions to the north and the southward flowing Indonesian Flowthrough Current (part of the World's Ocean Conveyor – a massive system of currents that circulates oceanic water right around the world taking about 32 years to do so), arid inland to the east, warm waters of the Leeuwin Current to the west and the temperate arid conditions to the south. As a consequence the area has low rainfall, high evaporation rates and relatively high temperatures and is subject to summer cyclones. The offshore and near shore conditions are moderated due to the influences of the Indian Ocean and currents from the north.

Depending on your references the area is described variously as arid or semi-arid leading east and north into desert. Least rain occurs in the period September to November with an average of less than 5mm per month and an annual average of about 300mm or less. The occasional cyclonic event may lead to extreme rainfall producing enough rain to exceed the annual average in a day! Dryness is the norm with up to 20 thunderstorms in any one place during the summer period.

This is a hot region with an average of 320 days of sunshine per year and with summer average daily temperatures reaching more than 33°C on the coast in February and March, the hottest months, getting down to an average just under 24°C at night with inland temperatures usually about 8°C hotter. During winter, temperatures moderate with a daily average maximum of 23°C and minimum average of 15°C in the coolest month of July. Cold air masses from the south will often drop temperatures dramatically.

Winds are calmest during the autumn and winter months. SW winds with an average 35km/hr inshore predominate in spring and summer and much stronger offshore. Winter winds tend to be much more variable, dominated by southerlies at similar speeds. Southeasterlies tend to be the predominant autumn winds but they are highly variable.

Cyclones have occurred in the region from December to May but usually are most common in February and March. A cyclone crosses the Shark Bay - Ningaloo Coast about every two years with an extreme one every 25 years on average. They often travel quite a way inland. As you move further south cyclones tend to have less effect and are less regular.

LEN ZELL

The wreck of the *Mildura* at Point Murat is one of many ships caught in the complex weather and currents of this coast.

Oceanography

Stromatolites survive in extreme
marine conditions. Hamelin Pool.

Currents

LEN ZELL

Ocean and coastal currents tend to be driven by the pull of the moon, oceanic drift and to a lesser extent wind, tides, temperature and salinity in decreasing effect. Two primary currents drive the systems in this area. The stronger of the two, the Leeuwin Current flows at up to 3 knots (5km/hr) south along the continental shelf all year, is about 50km wide and 200m deep and strongest in March to April slowing over winter and weakest in summer. It is the world's longest current reaching right around to Tasmania and drives most of Western Australia's weather (Ridgway and Costin, 2004). Being a low salinity, low nutrient and warm current, it

There are many great snorkelling opportunities along the Ningaloo Reef coast - Bundegi.

brings marine life from the north and allows survival of tropical species much further south. As the shelf is narrowest adjacent to Ningaloo Reef, it is here the Leeuwin Current bounces off the coast. Because it has big swirls and eddies up to several hundreds of kilometres across in addition to its southerly run, sometimes there can be ocean water floods into Shark Bay.

There is also a southward flowing 'Indonesian Flowthrough' which is part of the world's Ocean Conveyor Belt of currents. This current is also very important in bringing larvae of many species from the world's 'Coral Triangle' (including Indonesia, Malaysia, through to Papua New Guinea and the Solomon Islands), which has the world's highest marine diversity of species.

A colder counter-current heads northwards under the Leeuwin. Some of these colder waters are dragged up by northerly winds driving waters along the coast until the Ningaloo Current full flow is established in spring to mid-autumn. It flows between the front of the reefs and edge of the continental shelf, out to where the Leeuwin Current operates. Strong winds for an extended period can reverse the surface currents for short periods. Tidal currents create strong flows inside Ningaloo Reef and through the passages into and out of the reef as the tide changes.

As a result of all these local and further afield influences the Shark Bay - Ningaloo Coast tends to be well circulated. Shark Bay and its reaches and Exmouth Gulf are exceptions as they tend to be tidally circulated only. The current flows allow the systems to build up and maintain nutrients and larvae within them. This leads to the high productivity we see in these, generally low nutrient, waters of this oceanic coast.

Water temperatures

The sea surface temperatures range from a low of 19°C in winter to 26°C in summer and maxima of 24°C to 31°C respectively. As we go further south they decrease.

Water depths

There is a sudden drop off into the Indian Ocean depths of more than 5000m, 80km offshore near North West Cape (See Map page 73). Here the continental shelf is 12km wide and this is the closest land to the edge of the continental shelf in Australia. To the north and south the continental shelf widens until its widest point on this coast off Shark Bay at over 120km. Where the shelf is narrow, the ocean currents and deep-water surges have a greater coastal effect leading to interesting phenomena like aggregations of bait fish which are then fed on by sharks, whales and pelagic (open water) species of fish. In addition, migrating species such as Humpback Whales, will be seen closer to shore as well. In Shark Bay depths vary from 11m and shoal into beaches and shallow intertidal flats. Exmouth Gulf is over 20m at the mouth and in the middle, shelving into the salt flats and mangroves.

Tides

Tides along the Ningaloo Reef and Shark Bay coasts range from, in the north, 2.75m at Exmouth, 1.85m at Coral Bay, 1.8 at Carnarvon, 1.7 at Denham and 2.4 at Monkey Mia. Tides are variable, often with only one tide per day in Shark Bay due to the enclosed waters, becoming regular and diurnal to the north where there are two highs and two lows every day.

Tsunamis

There are indications of tsunamis occurring regularly in this area with about four in the last 120 years. These are commonly called tidal waves but have nothing to do with tides. They are caused by slumping of massive rock and mud off the continental shelf or earthquakes and the active shifting of tectonic plates of the Earth's surface crust, especially near Indonesia to the north. A tsunami hit between Coral Bay and North West Cape in 1994 travelling several hundred metres inland near Yardie Creek due to the breaks in the reef offshore. These events can carry marine sediments and organisms well inshore and wash terrestrial sediments and species offshore. They can cause significant damage to towns and coastal populations which could be why the Aboriginal people stayed away from some coastal areas.

Salinity

Salinity of the region is usually that of normal sea water with the slightly lower salinity of the currents offshore. Coastal runoff is spasmodic due to the low rainfall interspersed with dramatic cyclonic outputs. When these occur the fresh water floats on top of the seawater and slowly intermixes over a period of days. A significant amount of freshwater would be 'leaking' into the sea from the underground water systems but these amounts are unknown. Several bays in the Shark Bay complex are poorly circulated and as a consequence we see hypersaline conditions established where the salinity reaches double that of normal sea water.

Human Discovery, Naming and Use

The original discovery and settlement of this coast was by Aboriginal people thousands of years ago whereas the colonisation by the British in the last 200 years – was less "discovery" and more "invasion". With the arrival of Europeans in their country, Aboriginal people saw the disintegration of their cultures. The Europeans took over their land for grazing or mining with little regard for them as people with a culture.

When Europeans arrived in Australia there were more than 600 different Aboriginal languages, from about 30 traditional language groups spoken throughout Australia. There are only about 100 languages left and they are in great danger of disappearing. It is most appropriate that we regard the region and people of each language as a nation. Each of these nations had their own culture, oral histories and traditions. Their languages are as sophisticated as other modern languages and, some argue better, because of their ability to describe whole situations with a single word – a system very difficult for most to understand.

Unfortunately Aboriginal people were generally treated as inferior and books like *Jandamarra and the Bunuba Resistance* and *Yammatji – Aboriginal Memories of the Gascoyne* reinforce the inappropriate treatment of these people, the massive numbers who died from diseases and the appalling methods used to remove them from their land. These texts are a mere inkling of what occurred whilst the data collected on their culture and society was miniscule, often just a few notes or two or three scattered articles for one tribal group. "The tragedy is that, even today, few white Australians are aware of or appreciate the genius of Aboriginal culture" – *The Jigalong Mob*.

Within the lands of this text, R & C Berndt's book *Aborigines of the West - Their Past and Their Present* states, that 'the local traditional cultures are no longer a living reality'. This was due to the people dying of disease, being killed off or relocating out of their country attracted by food at the missions or pastoral stations, mining operations or pearling fleets including their indentured labour systems. This also resulted in the amalgamation of several, or many, groups into one. Nonetheless, through their birth right linkages to particular tracts of land, or 'country' as it is known, and through birth, law, religion, traditional and sacred sites, usually the responsibility of the men to maintain, the Aboriginal people have maintained strong cultural threads.

K. Forrest in her preface to *The Challenge and the Chance* outlines the horror for Aboriginal people,

> "from the time Western Australia gained full control of Aboriginal administration in 1898 to the period of the First World War, devastating anti-Aboriginal legislation altered the legal status of Aborigines. Divided from the main stream of society by a rigid Government system, controlled by public servants, denied the right to work by an implacable labour force and with no citizenship rights, the once free and proud Aboriginal race rapidly deteriorated. The ignorance, racial prejudice and indifference of the white community hastened their decline".

Each nation would generally intermarry with neighbouring nations following very specific kinship rules. Their languages had exceptional structure, extensive vocabularies and grammar equal to the Middle Eastern and classical European languages.

The Aboriginal people, especially the women, have encyclopaedic knowledge of the 'bush tucker' of the region. The foods obtained by careful collection, leaching, fermenting and cooking often have strong religious or ceremonial importance as well. In addition their knowledge of seasonal cycles and indicator species for when certain foods are available all demonstrate a sophisticated ability to live well in an apparently hostile land. Those European explorers who arrogantly ignored the knowledge and skills of the Aboriginal people often died under a tree rich in foods not far from a spring of sweet water.

Archaeological evidence along the coast, so far collected, dates the occupation of North West Cape at over 32,000 years, the oldest records of a maritime based culture in Australia, and Shark Bay over 5000 years. Evidence is found in the form of artefacts from caves, shell middens, rock shelters and quarries. The occupation dates of Shark Bay are relatively recent considering Aboriginal occupation of Australia dates back over 40,000 years. This is to be expected as the groups moved with rising sea levels so that many sites are now well underwater out to the 130m depth contour.

LEN ZELL

Caves in Cape Range exhibit petroglyphs that may have special significance.

Tribal groups around Shark Bay included the Nanda to the south of Shark Bay, the Inngarda to the east and the Wadjari, well to the east inland and all understood the Amangu people's dialect who lived in the Carnarvon area with the Malgana people living in central Shark Bay which they called Cartharrugudu. The settlement of Carnarvon in the late 1800s was in the middle of the land area occupied by the Mandi clan. Many Aboriginal people still live in and around Carnarvon and on the Mungullah Aboriginal Community. The Baijungu occupied the coast around Point Quobba, the Maia to their south and the Jinigudira the North West Cape peninsula. The Gnulli people are the custodians of the North West Cape. Another well-known Aboriginal Community in the Gascoyne is the Burringurrah Aboriginal Community about 30kms from Burringurrah (Mt Augustus) which is near the northernmost boundary of their traditional lands.

As colonisation occurred and many Aboriginal people died from disease or were killed, those who survived were dispossessed from their land and placed in missions, leading to the disintegration of their societies and culture. Many then lived and worked on pastoral stations, prior to the awarding of equal wages in the 60s. This decision saw the exodus of Aboriginal people from the stations, where they were often no longer wanted, to towns. The formation of many Aboriginal communities not run by white bureaucrats is an attempt to regain some dignity and reclaim what is left of their history and culture. As you travel the coast and pathways you will see many signs to Aboriginal settlements where they have begun this process.

Aboriginal use of the coastal areas changed as the sea levels rose and fell and as the edge of the continental shelf is close to the coast near North West Cape it was easy for them to have maintained a presence here regardless of sea level height. There are no traditional members of the original tribe living on the Cape, although there are living elders from other groups who act as custodians for this "lost tribe". According to Tindale, this group was the Jinigudira, who lived in the mangroves on the eastern side of the Exmouth Gulf.

Accounts from books like *The Wreck of the Barque Stephano* showed that Aboriginal people used Ningaloo Reef (Ningaloo - aboriginal meaning "nose") as a food resource. There were abundant molluscs, fish, turtles, turtle eggs and dugong that could be eaten. They were recorded as being friendly and gentle people who quite readily helped the shipwrecked sailors to survive in this harsh arid environment. Caves and rock shelters throughout the region have remarkable and extensive painting, petroglyphs and stencils. With the destruction of much of the Aboriginal cultures many of the stories and meanings of this 'art' have been lost. Should you ask an Aboriginal what something means it is not possible for them to tell us as we have not been initiated to the level that allows us to know that information.

Aboriginal people used 'firestick farming' extensively, which probably led to the parkland-like landscape that the early Europeans saw and painted. Today we have no good records of how often and how much was burnt in those times. This means we are confronted with a continuing dilemma of where to burn and when. If we don't burn, fuel loads build up and then we have very severe fires rather than the more sedate forms seen by Dampier, Cook and others. The mosaic burning pattern developed by the Aboriginal methods is proposed as the best fire management practice to be used today.

Recorded European history in the Gascoyne dates back some 400 years. Others believe the Chinese mapped Australia in the 1400s (*1421* by Gavin Menzies), and others as far back as 2000 years BC – see *Columbus Was Last*. The Dutch were the first to record landing along the Gascoyne coast in the early 1600s and many of the names of places and towns along the coast provide a lasting legacy of those early explorers. We also wonder about those who came here and left no records, and like the Portuguese, were not to tell anyone, under the pain of excommunication or death, of their knowledge of sea routes.

Dirk Hartog made the first recorded European landing in Shark Bay at Cape Inscription in 1616. He was followed by William Jansz in the *Mauritius* who landed at North West Cape in 1618. William Vlamingh landed on this coast in 1697 and was followed two years later by the first Englishman, William Dampier. He named Shark Bay because of all the sharks he saw. Dampier's cook died while they were in Shark Bay and was the first recorded European to be buried in Australia.

The French explorer Francois St. Allouran arrived and claimed Australia for France at Cape Inscription in 1772. He buried 2 French coins and a parchment in a bottle to support his claim – they have not been found. Two French naval ships – the *Geographe* and *Naturaliste* - led by Nicolas Baudin on a scientific expedition to the WA coast, first in 1801 and then again in 1803, named many places and undertook a lot of important discovery work for Australia. Captain Hamelin of the *Naturaliste* found and repaired de Vlamingh's plate at Cape Inscription and added one to commemorate Baudin's expedition. Louis de Freycinet had been a member of Baudin's expedition and returned here in 1818 on the *Uranie* to continue the exploratory work. He removed de Vlamingh's plate to France. It returned to Australia in 1947 and can be seen in the Maritime Museum in Fremantle.

Captain Denham charted Shark Bay in 1858 carving *"Denham; Herald 1858"* into a cliff at Eagle Bluff. This carved section is now in Denham's Pioneer Park.

The Aboriginal name for Shark Bay is Catharruguda (Two Bays). Cape Peron and Francois Peron National Park (Baudin after the naturalist on French *Geographe* in 1801-1803) are two of the many sites here named by Baudin.

Commercial pastoralism and pearling started in and near Shark Bay area from the 1860s with all the land taken up by the 1880s. Today about 85% of the region is used by pastoralists.

Pearling settlements were dotted along the coast using Malay and Aboriginal people for labour, with Chinese boats tending to use their own people. Much of the pearling along the Western Australian coast used enslaved Aboriginal divers because of their diving abilities. The magnificent luggers were the core of the pearling industry with hundreds at a time operating along this coast; sadly very few of them are left. This is an industry with some great tales some of which are recorded in *Redbill* by Kate Lance.

Guano mining occurred on islands of Shark Bay in the mid 1800s with a small garrison placed on Dirk Hartog Island to try to prevent the volumes of guano being taken illegally

LEN ZELL

for Mauritius and the UK. Sandalwood harvesting began about this time as well.

The great Depression of the 1930s contributed to the demise of the pearling industry, with the manufacture of bakelite and plastics also taking their toll before WWII took all the boats. The industry partly recovered but it wasn't until the cultured pearl industry developed that there was a resurgence of success. The wool industry is still a major contributor to the economy of the region.

Whaling was begun by Americans after 1790 with land-based operations undertaken along this coast from the early 1900s, and they were too successful, killing off the whale stocks so that operations at all sites finished in the 1970s. Important locations were Point Cloates and Norwegian Bay. Using factory ships and chaser boats the target species were initially Sperm Whales then Humpbacks with up to 2500 Humpbacks taken annually in the late 1930s.

Commercial fisheries and the construction of a processing factory and cannery boosted the economy of Shark Bay from 1912 and is still a major contributor today. The factory was originally on Herald Bight on the Peron Peninsula with the remains now being a tourist attraction.

Monkey Mia is now famous for its dolphins, which have provided a major addition to the framework for a thriving tourist industry in Shark Bay. The main Shark Bay town of Denham (after Captain H.H. Denham who charted Shark Bay in 1858) acts as an accommodation base and harbour for many users of the bay.

Lieutenant George Grey explored and named the Gascoyne River in 1839 during his explorations inland and along much of this coast. Twenty years later Frank Gregory, after whom the Gregory Ranges are named, explored much more of the region and inland to Burringurrah (Mt Augustus). The district of Carnarvon (after the British Secretary of State, Lord Carnarvon) was not settled until the 1880s and the establishment of telegraphic communications to Perth in 1884 helped reduce its isolation. "One Mile Jetty" built in 1897 established Carnarvon as the "hub" of the Gascoyne and is now one of the main tourist attractions of the town.

Gold was discovered 35 years after Robert Austin's explorations of the region in 1854. He reported that there was significant evidence for minerals inland. Mt Magnet, Cue, Sandstone and Meekatharra then all boomed as more people came in and exploited the region. Gold has remained the primary focus for the existence of these towns and many smaller ones that didn't survive to the present. A railway was built from

The old railway siding at the Nannine township site rings with history.　LEN ZELL

Charles Knife Canyon is incised into the Cape Range limestones.　LEN ZELL

the coast to Meekatharra and Sandstone in the late 1800s and closed in the late 1970s.

A shocking experiment was conducted on Dorre and Bernier Islands in 1904 where all Aboriginal people suffering from any venereal disease or leprosy were brought from hundreds of kilometres away throughout NW WA and interned on the islands. Fortunately this was ceased in 1911. It was thought this would prevent further spread of the diseases when it appears that all it did was bring pain to many unfortunate people.

Prior to the establishment of Exmouth for military purposes, the settlement of North West Cape came from the pastoral industry, World War II, and the oil industry. Situated between Coral Bay and Exmouth is the originally titled Point Cloates Station now known as Ningaloo Station which was the first established (and still operating) pastoral station on this coast.

LEN ZELL

Commercial fishers catch tonnes of whiting each year.

Construction of the Vlamingh Head lighthouse (Captain de Vlamingh - Dutch) in 1912, was too late to save the SS *Mildura* wrecked here in 1907. She was carrying building materials and about 400 bullocks. You can still see the remains of the wreck off Point Murat. The lighthouse, which was decommissioned in 1967 with one of the VLF towers of the Communications Base replacing it, has now been extensively restored as a tourist attraction.

On the eastern side of North West Cape, Exmouth Gulf (Phillip Parker King after Viscount Exmouth, Edward Pellew) is an important area for prawn fisheries with a fleet based at the Exmouth harbour and near Learmonth. Several pearl aquaculture ventures operated in the Gulf with fish aquaculture developing. The Bay of Rest (Phillip Parker King 1818 - Jogador is Aboriginal name) is a popular fishing and recreational area for the locals.

Exmouth, gazetted in 1963, was opened by Prime Minister Harold E Holt in 1967. It was built by the US and Australian Governments as a support town for the Harold E Holt Naval Communications Base. Originally a military town, it is now an international gateway for Ningaloo Reef. Exmouth's population has waxed and waned from 4500 to now between 2000 and 2500. After the departure of most of the US personnel, Exmouth has become reliant on the tourist dollar, with whale sharks, reef diving and fishing being the primary drawcards.

Between Learmonth and Exmouth the Charles Knife and Shothole Canyon Roads cut clear scars on the landscape leading into the magnificent scenery of Cape Range. These roads are a testament to the oil exploration drilling that occurred in Rough Range and Cape Range in the 1950s. Some tour operators also offer tours traversing the Cape Range from east to west.

This area still stirs interest from the mining sector, with major companies over the last 15 years successfully pursuing the hunt for "liquid gold" in the form of oil on North West Cape, around the Muiron Islands and successfully within 50kms of the coast. Fortunately mining and oil exploration is not allowed in Ningaloo Marine Park. No significant discoveries have been made on land, with the economically viable reserves being found below the seabed some 30-50km offshore. These reserves are being developed and oil is taken from an anchored Floating Production, Storage and Offshore (FPSOs) Loading facilities to markets overseas. Mining such as this provides little to the economy of the region, does not provide employment for the local community and increases the potential of oil spills no matter how small, in the region,.

Other mining operations that contribute significantly to the economy are the salt and gypsum productions at Lake MacLeod and Useless Loop. The Gascoyne Region "harvests" over one quarter of Western Australia's salt. One company proposed to develop a massive evaporative salt operation on the eastern side of Exmouth Gulf. This was not approved by the EPA. There are regionally significant stands of mangroves (6 species) and ancient algal mats in the location so logic should prevent the proposal succeeding. These are also, as yet unprotected areas, that will suffer catastrophically should there be an oil spill.

It's a case of "Reward versus risk" – reward for the miners but risk for Ningaloo Reef and environs, which provide the natural resource around which a growing tourist industry has developed. Tourism is now one of the greatest economic contributors to the Gascoyne Region, with the Shark Bay and Ningaloo Coast World Heritage Areas being the two rapidly growing drawcards for national and international visitors. Outback tourism and travellers passing through also continue to grow well.

Recently a survey has indicated that the whole region from Onslow to just south of Geraldton, out to sea including the Perth Basin and Exmouth Gulf areas and inland to Mt Keith is about to undergo significant growth in mining. (Weekend Australian 13-14 Nov 2004). Some 24 major projects are yielding more than $10million per year and employ about one sixth of the region's 32,000 with 10,000 more in flow-on effects. The outlook is for minerals, oil and gas to all expand as exploration and markets drive the growth. Is this sustainable and compatible with the other uses of the region?

Aboriginal 'Art' or what?

We find the term 'Art Sites' inappropriate or 'Aboriginal Art' for non-commercial pieces produced for sale as being realistic (although many of these commercially produced pieces still have stories that could arguably take them out of the realm of Art). The works of Aboriginals were for law, lore, passports, messages and so much more that we, the unitiated, will never be allowed to know. Nonetheless we will continue to use the term art but in quotation marks to indicate this issue.

ART defined from www.dictionary.reference.com/browse/art

NOUN 1. the quality, production, expression, or realm, according to aesthetic principles, of what is beautiful, appealing, or of more than ordinary significance.

Aboriginal 'Art' Forms of Shark Bay, Ningaloo and Outback Pathways

Paintings, petroglyphs, dance, wooden and fibre artefacts and decorated weapons or ceremonial items were highly complex visual devices, a means for Aboriginal people to support religious, law and family issues, as maps or to enhance the oral aspect of their society. These stories and the art wove the fabric by which they lived. Some sites are for men, some for women, some all people and so on. Then there were the mobile pieces used as passports to allow transit through a neighbouring group's land including what food to collect or hunt and at what times. Others were a call to battle and where

Mangrove roots and pneumatophores, samphire and mudflats are particularly susceptible to oil spills as any oil will coat and kill them.

LEN ZELL

to meet.

Due to our non-Aboriginal understanding of the 'art,' we tend to show interest in the more spectacular forms and less interest in the less spectacular, how they fitted into the society of those who performed this 'art' and what the pieces really mean .

Most of the 'art' in this region was used for many purposes and does not compare well with the dramatic Wandjina, Gwion Gwion and Arnhem Land forms to the north. As a consequence most of the pieces of this region are generally poorly known and most stories behind them are lost. One port development destroyed a whole major site of petroglyphs.

Generally non-Aboriginal peoples have little capacity to understand the complexity of these graphic systems as they are so foreign to our way of thinking. As a consequence our arrival at a site, often past carefully placed 'signpost stones,' meant to keep all or one sex or age group out, is often inappropriate. Sometimes at these sites taking photographs, laughing or talking etc. can be deemed to be totally inappropriate – as it would be in the holiest of holy locations in a church or similar religious site.

Throughout this region there are petroglyphs, ochre paintings, stencils, rock arrangements and carved trees. Rock 'art' is dependent on suitable rock surfaces on which to paint or carve.

We do not publish any photographs of the 'art' seen as it could be highly insulting or distressing to the people who know it. Should you see any 'art' then please treat it with absolute respect.

Major Habitats

The underwater world of
seagrasses are rich

Marine and Intertidal Habitats

Open Ocean

This coast is part of all the world's oceans – all interconnected and generally biologically known as part of the Indo-Pacific system, as the colder waters to the north and south of these oceans prevent species moving into the Atlantic. Prevailing currents will determine which marine life will be present in the open oceans. Warm, nutrient rich waters will provide an ideal environment for the floating microscopic plants (phytoplankton) that in turn provide food for the floating microscopic animals (zooplankton) – including larval stages of many larger animals, that provide food for the bigger animals right up the food chain to the top predators such as mackerel, tuna, billfish, sharks and dolphins. The Whale Sharks feed on the small planktonic organisms and congregate in this area during the breeding or spawning times of the coral reef animals. Generally off this coast we find low nutrient waters with a lower salinity so efficiency is necessary for the reef systems to capture anything they can from these waters. Pelagic species (free swimming in the ocean) include mackerel, billfish and tuna with the demersal species (mid water to bottom) of snapper, emperors, perch and then benthic (bottom) species of goatfish and the like. Whales, dolphins and turtles also frequent these areas with only some of the dolphin species being 'resident'.

Manta rays and other large plankton feeders   LEN ZELL
like Whale Sharks come in to feast on the massive amounts
of coral spawn released each year on 'the night'.

Seabeds - outer shelf or continental slopes

These tend to be usually less rich in life due to the lack of light, suitable substrates and nutrients, as they range from about 150m to 800m deep. They are presently poorly known in this region. Nonetheless they are amazing habitats deserving special attention as there are enormous numbers of bizarre animals that rely on the food that floats down from above. These include sponges, worms, crustaceans and molluscs. The substrate tends to be oozes of fine mud and some sand.

Seabeds - inner or continental shelf

This is a limestone shelf overlain with sand and mud washed off the mainland and deposited there as the sea rose at the end of the last ice age. Here we find many more fish, crustaceans (especially prawns and crayfish) and many mollusc (marine snails) species due to the inflow of nutrients from the shore. Intermixed with these are rich soft coral, algae, sponge and seastar communities. Trawling targets these waters and has a dramatically damaging impact on the life found here. The shelf is narrowest at Point Cloates, being only 5km wide and then widens slightly to the north and to about 35km off Cape Farquhar and over 120km at Cape Inscription.

Seabeds - reef lagoon

Between the mainland and reefs making up the Ningaloo Reef complex, and some areas to the south, there tends to be a shallow lagoon which is usually sandy floored, sometimes

ich coral patches can be found on the outer reef edges, and in the shallower inshore
goons, all can be wiped out by a single cyclonic event.

LEN ZELL

Careful examination of the surfaces of seagrass yields views of algae and many animals.   LEN ZELL

scoured by currents, with occasional exposures of the ancient limestone rocks under thin layers of sand. They are interesting spots to snorkel but watch those currents! Here are found sea cucumbers, shells, sand feeding fish, rays or if you are lucky enough a passing Dugong!

Seabeds - seagrass meadows

Shark Bay's seagrass meadows are the biggest in the world and can be seen from space or by looking out from almost any beach in the whole Shark Bay area. They support an extremely important Dugong population of about 10,000 animals - more than 10% of the world's population. The seagrasses are flowering plants and their beds tend to not only be highly productive in their own right but also provide a substrate and shelter for an enormous diversity of small animals and other plants. Each seagrass plant is covered by hundreds of small algae, diatoms, forams and other microscopic organisms. Prawns, seastars, larval fish and crustaceans can be found amongst the plants.

Boat propellers, coastal runoff and cyclones are the primary damaging actions affecting these meadows. The masses of seagrasses often seen washed up on beaches also play an important role in the energy and nutrient cycles by providing a massive input of food for bacteria, fungi and grazing copepods and amphipods, which all break it down into small particles or chemicals to be recycled.

Oil Spills

Generally the highest impacts of oil spills will be on seabirds, turtles and especially intertidal communities, such as mangroves, which will get coated by the oil. This is an issue Australia will struggle with as the enormous pressure to develop the Carnarvon, Canning and Browse Basins offshore for oil and gas increases.

Limestone rock forms little cliffs all along the Ningaloo Coast.   LEN ZELL

Intertidal - rocky shores

Limestone is the primary rock found on the shores along this coast. As a consequence we tend not to see rich oyster communities as maybe the rock tends to degrade too quickly or the environment is wrong. Algae and many molluscs are common, with zonation occurring due to the differing spray and splash zones. Overhangs, pools, blowholes, caves and crevices provide an enormous number of different habitats and hiding places from the elements and predators.

ivid blue staghorn colonies are uncommon but stand out dramatically for snorkellers. hey contain a very strong natural sunscreen but are very susceptible to higher than ormal temperatures which cause them to bleach to a vivid white then die.

LEN ZELL

A sandy beach leads into the shallow lagoon and nearby reef top. Ningaloo Reef.   LEN ZELL

Intertidal – sandy shores

Windblown limestone sands from old marine sediments and coral reefs and some siliceous sands make up these habitats. Take time to look at the sand grains carefully to see if you can tell where they came from. Turn your binoculars around for a microscopic look. Many small animals known as interstitial fauna live between the sand grains and are too small for us to see, so are generally are poorly known. Crabs, worms and shells also abound. Please do not collect shells – even dead ones – as they provide homes for hermit crabs. A walk up from the beach into the dunes on the designated walkways may let you see remains of old cyclone placed sands or dunes developed by strong prevailing winds.

Nesting turtles, the occasional bird and many other animals use these beaches to hatch their young with many animals foraging along the shore especially wading birds, foxes, crabs, Dingoes and small mammals. Watch for their tracks and see if you can work out what was happening.

Turtles

LEN ZELL

Turtles dawdle throughout the Shark Bay - Ningaloo Coast, with several species nesting on many of the island and mainland beaches. Females come ashore to lay their eggs in a specially dug egg chamber, but only if the sand has a suitable temperature and moisture content. Each will lay from 50-150 eggs depending on species and on which one of her 3-5 layings she will do in any one season - since she may not lay again for 2-11 years. The young hatch, after about seven weeks, and as a group dig to just below the surface to wait for cool, dark conditions. Then they emerge and dash for the sea. Gulls, herons, fish, sharks and other large predators catch many and less than 1% will survive to maturity.

Turtle Watching Codes of Conduct

MATING TURTLES

- If in a boat watch from a distance of at least 50m and be as still and quiet as possible.
- Do not approach any closer than 50m for any reason.
- If snorkelling approach to where you can just see them and then no closer.

NESTING FEMALES

SUSIE BEDFORD

Hatchling turtles emerge from their nest.

- Ask the Rangers when and where the best turtle watching will be.

- Arrive at the carpark quietly and slowly while dimming or turning off car headlights as soon as possible.

- Carry a low powered torch (3w bulb or less, preferably a red light), shoes, jumper and water to drink.

- At the top of the beach wait for about 10 minutes to let your eyes get used to the dark with no lights on. Once you have your night vision YOU DO NOT NEED A TORCH. If you do use a torch it will chase the nesting females back into the sea.

- Move along the high tide mark watching for turtle tracks (about 1m across) in the sand.

- If you see a turtle emerging – freeze and watch one of the most amazing experiences of your life as she makes her way up the beach past you – be quiet and in particular be very still as turtles are sensitive to movement. Wait until she finds a spot to start digging – this may takes minutes or sometime.

- Once you find a nesting turtle only approach from behind. If you get hit by flying sand you are far too close and she is not ready to be approached.

- If conditions are not right or you frighten her she will abandon the attempt. Once she has dug the egg chamber using her hind flippers only, she will start to lay. Once she has started to lay it is possible to approach closely from behind to watch but AVOID THE USE OF FLASH PHOTOGRAPHY.

- Once finished laying, she needs space to cover her nest and then get back to the water. DO NOT approach closely during these times.

- Leave the beaches by 11pm letting the turtles have the rest of the night to themselves.

- If visiting Exmouth, visit the Jurabi Turtle Centre for guided night time tours or contact DEC for more information on the Ningaloo Community Turtle Monitoring Program (www.ningalooturtles.org.au - a joint project between Cape Conservation Group Inc (CCG), and DEC) run from November through to March. They are always looking volunteers – training is provided.

- Stand well away from the nests to ensure you do not crush the young who will be a few cms below the surface.

- Do not use lights at all.

- Let the hatchlings make their own way to the beach.

- Keep footprints above the nests as they can trap hatchlings.

Dunes

These occur along all the beaches and then there are the fossilised ones inland. The amount of minerals attached to the white grains will determine their colours.

Mudflats and Estuaries - Marine Wetlands

Mudflats and Estuaries are fabulous areas of very harsh conditions for animals and plants. They tend to go from one extreme to another – salt water to fresh water and wet to dry all in minutes and this all overlain with rushing or gentle water flows.

Mobile dunes can be seen along the Ningaloo Coast.   LEN ZELL

Mangroves

Unlike other flowering plants, mangroves are trees that have adapted to living in intertidal areas. These amazing plants have neat ways of dealing with salty water, which periodically covers their root systems and yet they still require fresh water either from a stream flow or percolating up through the substrate. Some have "salt filters", which prevent salt entering the plant through the roots, some have developed salt glands in their leaves to extrude the salt and others concentrate salt in "sacrificial" leaves and bark which removes the salt as they fall off the tree.

Patterns of species occurrences known as zonation can be seen. This is due to the differing levels of sea water from tidal inundations, the salinity tolerances of the species, mud density and evaporation rates.

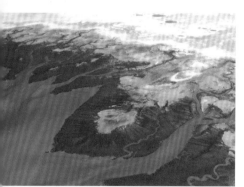

Rich mangrove communities and mudflats fringe Exmouth Gulf.   TERRY DONE

Some mangroves have floating seeds to aid their dispersal. Many grow into a fully developed small plant, or propagule, that drops off the tree into water to remain dormant until it finds its way into the mud and is ready to grow, with shoots and roots emerging. The pencil shaped seeds are designed to drop off and spear into the mud below – developing into a new mangrove.

The leaf litter that accumulates on the mud is broken down by the crabs that live in the mud and then further decomposed by masses of bacteria. This helps to recycle nutrients within the mangrove ecosystem and provides nutrients to nearby rivers, sea, reef and seagrass ecosystems. The mud is usually lacking oxygen (anaerobic) and production of hydrogen sulphide by the bacteria gives rise to the "rotten egg" smell often associated with mangroves.

In order to cope with this lack of oxygen in the mud, mangroves have developed fascinating strategies for dealing with this problem – they stick part of their root systems in the air! Some have "pneumatophores" – little pencil or peg roots that stick vertically out of the ground, others have stilt, prop and knee roots. All these aerial roots "suck in" oxygen through lenticels – special "breathing" cells that have holes, which close when covered with water to prevent seawater entering the roots.

These amazing aerial root systems provide a tangled refuge for many small marine animals at high tide. Consequently mangroves are known as nursery areas for many organisms because the juveniles can seek shelter from much larger predators that patrol the fringes of the mangroves. Hence mangrove communities are very important for commercial and recreational fisheries. The mangroves on the eastern side of Exmouth Gulf are significant nursery areas for the prawns which form the basis of the Exmouth Gulf prawn fishery. Any activities which affect these mangrove communities would have significant impact on all fisheries.

From the Bay of Rest around to the eastern side of Exmouth Gulf are regionally significant stands of mangroves, with 6 species on the eastern side. Only 3 species are found in the mangrove communities or mangals along the Ningaloo Reef coastline - at Mangrove Bay and Yardie Creek. The 3 species are the Grey or White Mangrove, the Red or Spider Mangrove and Ribbed Mangrove, with the Grey Mangrove being the dominant species. A small community of mangroves in the Bundegi Sanctuary, a few kilometres north of Exmouth, is mainly the Grey Mangrove, with only 1 Red Mangrove tree.

Conditions found around North West Cape are not really conducive for mangrove growth because of the lack of suitable substrates and low rainfall. Mangroves thrive in tropical conditions with higher rainfall. It appears that the flow of underground water into Mangrove Bay and the fresh water at Yardie Creek maintained these communities, which may have been more extensive, but as the area became more arid the mangroves communities have shrunk.

Shark Bay is the only other place along the Gascoyne Coast that has mangroves, although these are not as diverse as the Ningaloo or Gulf communities. They appear as small isolated communities in the southern and western parts of Shark Bay. Scientific evidence of mangrove related fossils indicates that the distribution of mangroves along the Gascoyne coast, between 4000 – 6000 years ago would have been far more extensive than the current distribution. This would have been due to changing sea levels and wetter periods.

Mangrove Bay boardwalk and bird hide are excellent places to observe mangroves and the fauna associated with them. Take the time to look in the shallows to see fish, rays and crabs including the aggressive blue swimmers and mud crabs. Mangrove Bay is in a sanctuary area within Ningaloo Marine Park so no taking of animals or plants is allowed - follow the well known phrase "Take nothing but photos, leave nothing but footprints".

It is very important that the intriguing aerial roots are not damaged as it could kill the trees, so tread carefully when walking around amongst them, should you ever need to. Take advantage of the boardwalk for a safe and non-damaging way of experiencing a mangrove community. Look for mudskippers peering out of holes and grazing on the muddy surface. Wait patiently and you will often see the fiddler crabs with brightly coloured claws trying unobtrusively to creep out of their holes to wave their claws for territory marking or mating – ready to scurry back down at the slightest hint of movement.

In the bird hide you will often see many different species of water bird ranging from pelicans, darters and cormorants, to ospreys and sea eagles calling and flying overhead. Look at the mangroves around the edge of the lagoon. You should be able to distinguish 2 very distinct colours of green – look for the darker patches of green that indicate the presence of the Red Mangrove. The lighter colour indicates the Grey Mangrove.

Try snorkelling around the roots of any mangroves at high tide. It is an eerie but fascinating experience - swimming amongst the schools of fish sheltering nervously amongst the roots with the shade of the trees giving dappled light effects. It is a totally different experience from snorkelling on a coral reef with its bright colours. Look for stingrays lying motionless in the shallows or shovelnose rays, which will swim rapidly away as you approach, or octopuses, the masters of camouflage, ready to change colour or shape when spotted or to squirt water at you if you venture too close.

Occasional rain will flood samphire flats – looking so much like a bonsai forest. These plants are only 60cm high.   LEN ZELL

Mangroves are very important ecologically so their conservation is critical. They are susceptible to pollution, especially oil, which covers their aerial roots and kills them. Oil companies involved in oil mining activities off the coast must have carefully planned Oil Response Plans in the event of an oil spill. As a tourist you need to ensure that your recreational activities do not affect these incredibly special trees. Destruction of mangroves starts a snowball effect which has far reaching consequences for us all. The Gascoyne coast mangroves are living on the edge of their "comfort zone" so any human activities can have major, dire effects.

Intertidal mudflats occur in most of the intertidal areas with some having extensive microbial mats such as in SE Exmouth Gulf. These flats can be rich soft mud, sandy mud, gritty mud or the like with some being metres deep and others a thin film over rock or sand underneath. Many of the mud flats can be used to see the history of the area and older sea levels. Often flats will occur above high water and these may be 15km wide and have incised creeks in them with a mangal fringe and samphire flats further inland. Often just landward of some flats there will be a beach ridge which could be from a higher sea level thousands of years ago or recent cyclonic events in the last few thousand years. Most flats have fauna distinctive to their area and animal diggings with burrows and conical mounds as they search for food.

Samphire flats

So called because of the fleshy "samphire" plants that often grow there, these salty alkaline environments occur throughout the region ranging from ephemeral landlocked pools to linear lakes which only fill from irregular rains and then the like of Lake MacLeod and the McNeill claypans at the mouth of the Gascoyne River and the supratidal systems in the southern Exmouth Gulf. The birridas, gypsum rich salt pans around Shark Bay add another dimension to this evaporational and salty environment. Grazing animals have had a much smaller impact on these systems when compared with the fresh water wetlands and pools.

Variations in vegetation cover range from totally bare pans to those with total cover and some with over 25 species present.

Intertidal - muddy shores/flats

Soft grey to brown muds abound in Exmouth Gulf and many of the estuarine areas especially near mangroves. These are often intermixed with layers of sand and other muds depending on what tidal, storm, river flow or other depositional activities have occurred over time. Intermixed with the muds are many algal species sometimes forming mats, burrowing worms, crabs, fish and other animals.

These can be highly productive areas biologically thus providing an important nutrient input into the whole system.

Algal blooms

LEN ZELL

Algal blooms occur regularly in coastal waters when temperatures, gas and nutrient levels are right. Blooms sometimes form slicks thousands of kilometres long. An enormous amount of biomass is produced and when it dies it can be toxic to marine life. (Often confused with 'coral spawn' and sometimes even with oil slicks – see box bit on coral Reproduction and Growth.)

Single celled, 2mm long, cigar shaped plants make up the algal blooms seen floating in tropical waters.

Islands

There are several primary island types along this coast – limestone cliffy islands with sand dunes covering them as on Dirk Hartog, sand dune islands like those in Exmouth Gulf, rocky islands like Bird Island in Shark Bay and the siliceous sand islands like Bernier and Dorre. All have important refuge status for many animals and some plants that have become extinct or threatened on the nearby mainland.

Nesting seabirds frequent many islands as they can be free of the predators found on the mainland and still be close to food sources. See the boxed bit on visiting these islands.

Hints for Visiting Nesting Bird Islands

LEN ZELL

Only go ashore if you know that it is OK – preferably with a guide.

Before you go ashore check that you have NO soil, seeds or animals attached to your clothing or shoes.

Stay below high tide mark and as close to the water as possible.

Keep together and quiet with slow cautious movements and watch the effects on the birds closely.

A Silver Gull quickly flies in and eats an egg exposed by an adult tern frightened away.

Ensure that you do not chase any adult nesting birds away from eggs or chicks as they can suffer from heat or be quickly devoured by the Silver Gulls which have learned that humans chase off the adults and make food available.

Reefs

The present sea level allowed new corals and plants to grow on the old fossil surfaces like icing on a cake. These are the coral reef systems we see today – all providing a matrix for more growth and erosion with habitats for countless other organisms. At the outer or seaward edge of the reef are species that can exist in these very tumultuous conditions. As we come up the face of the reef, the reef front exists with usually strong coral growth of rich communities, then onto the reef crest where we see an almost smooth surface covered by wave flattened corals and encrusting algae. Once past here the reef flat is again covered by corals and algae which tend to be less flattened forms and in small pools larger open colonies are maintained at a fixed height by exposure at average low tide height. This area then grades into pools and then loose coral heads, to the reef back which has beautiful coral gardens and isolated bommies, then into the sandy floors of the lagoons - often with seagrasses - then a gradual rise into the beaches.

Reef-building hard corals

LEN ZELL

These can be solitary or in colonies of animals. In the tissues of each animal (polyp) are single celled algae called *zooxanthellae*. These organisms capture carbon dioxide and the wastes from the coral polyps and through the process of photosynthesis, using energy from the sun, supply the coral with oxygen and sugars. Calcium carbonate is produced as a by-product of this photosynthetic process and each coral species dumps their wastes in a different shape, which we see as a skeleton. Coral bleaching occurs when seawater is too hot and excess oxygen is produced, becoming toxic to the coral. The corals then expel the zooxanthellae, losing their colour in the process (coral bleaching). If enough zooxanthellae are kept, the coral may survive. Often, complete expulsion means there aren't enough *zooxanthellae* to reseed the coral and it dies. Corals normally "spawn" once a year with an upside-down 'snowstorm of eggs and sperm' released into the water all at the same time. The next morning a pink slick appears as the eggs are fertilised and the larvae sink back to the bottom. Some such larvae may stay floating up to a month and travel hundreds of kilometres before settling.

On a calm day and with clear ocean waters washing over the reef top it is a snorkeller's dream. ...ich with colours, fish galore and such clarity – it is unusual.

LEN ZELL

Reef surfaces have an immense range of organisms and most of us suffer information overload after only a few minutes of exploration as a reef walker or snorkeller. If you take your time by staying still in one spot and concentrating on a small area you will be rewarded with fish, crabs and shells emerging to carry on their business that your arrival disturbed. Divers and snorkellers will have the opportunity to see the myriads of fish that inhabit coral reef waters with patient observers being able to see large numbers of different species with each dive.

Marine Research Efforts

Both the Federal and State Governments recognized the significance of Ningaloo Reef by providing millions of dollars in funding for the Ningaloo Research Program, an initiative of the Western Australian Marine Science Institute (WAMSI). To complement this research CSIRO established the Ningaloo Collaboration Cluster to address "the challenge of integrating the knowledge of reef use, biodiversity and socioeconomics into a management strategy for the Ningaloo Marine Park of Western Australia". The amount of oil and gas exploration in the area has hastened these decisions to attempt to get some baseline research completed should there be a blowout or similar.(www.csiro.au/partnerships/Ningaloo-Cluster.html#1).

In an attempt to ensure that the local community and other interested stakeholders have access to the research program results, the Ningaloo Atlas (www.ningaloo-atlas.org.au/) was established. It gives fascinating insights into the world of the reef and surrounds.

Spinifex clumps provide microhabitat for hundreds of animals.   LEN ZELL

Terrestrial Habitats

Grasslands

Introduced Buffel and natural spinifex are the predominant grass species found throughout the region. The spinifex clumps provide a complete habitat in itself. The grass clumps moderate the severe local conditions, with many animals and their predators living within and burrowing under them. Fire will reduce the area to bare earth with fast recovery, if enough moisture, and after rains.

Woodlands

Wattles, eucalypts, cypress pines, hakeas and poverty bush are the predominant woodland trees and shrubs. The density of these trees changes dramatically as you go through the transition from one soil type to another. This is often associated with sand dunes, riverine flats and other obvious changes. Sometimes the cause is much more subtle and will require extra examination. This is especially the case where the soils grade from limey sands into siliceous sands or underlying quartz country.

Note that in some areas there are total fire bans from November to March and heavy restrictions outside those times. So before you even consider a fire ensure that you are FULLY aware of the area's fire warning status – if in doubt don't, as the fines and effects of an out of control fire are enormous. Always check with the local authorities – see contacts in later chapter. Fires in National Parks are not permitted all year round.

LEN ZELL

Be prepared for wildlife crossing the road at all times.

Fire in habitats

LEN ZELL

Fire is today a natural aspect of the Australian landscape. It would have become common here millions of years ago as Australia drifted north away from Gondwana and became drier, with lightning strikes causing ignition. Aboriginal people used fire all year in a patchwork or mosaic-burning process. This allowed small areas to be burned rather than allowing the build-up of large areas of grass as fuel, which lead to more massively-destructive fires in the 'dry'. It would probably have taken many years to learn the best fire systems to use for food capture and ease of transit.

Fires can be extreme if fuel loads have been allowed to build up.

Today there is increasing knowledge of better management practices using fire which may see a return to the mosaic-burning system of the Aboriginal people. Most plants and animals are adapted to the mosaic system but not to severe bush fires across wider areas. If you wish to use a fire please ensure you follow all the DEC guidelines and be extremely careful.

Freshwater holes and Wetlands

There are many freshwater holes throughout the area both permanent and semi-permanent with a few spring fed. All have been extremely important for the Traditional Owners and then for the pastoralists who displaced them. The fauna of the region is highly dependent on these waters as well, with major effects occurring from the influx and use by stock and feral

animals. Many of the waterholes are degraded, especially by cattle, as grazing became more intense and we often see from the air tracks leading into waterholes looking like the slice lines in a pie. These tracks and camping stock have removed almost all of the understorey species around the waterholes.

Paperbarks, river gums and sedges are the predominant plants seen around some of the waterholes and various lilies and other water plants can be seen in them.

Clay pans are seldom used if there are freshwater holes in the streams nearby. About 60 species of waterbirds and 500 species of invertebrate fauna can be found in the freshwater lands of the region with numbers and species being heavily affected by the chemistry of the waters.

Placid waterholes were important both for the nomadic Aboriginals and then the droving stockmen.

LEN ZELL

Your exploration kit

You have to be totally self-sufficient wherever you go.

Minimal requirements include:

- Protective clothing of a cool broad-brimmed hat, cool long sleeves, sturdy shoes and strong socks or ideally long pants to protect against grass scratches, insects, snake bite or coral cuts.
- First aid kit and strong knife.
- A **minimum** of 4 litres of water per person per day and food. Dehydration is a major problem all year round.
- Maps, charts and tide tables.
- Communications with someone reliable nearby or who can organise local help.
- Sunscreen and insect repellent.
- EPIRB, compass, torch and reflecting mirror to attract attention of rescuers.
- Space blanket, matches and/or cigarette lighter.
- Camera to record the adventure and binoculars to watch the wildlife.

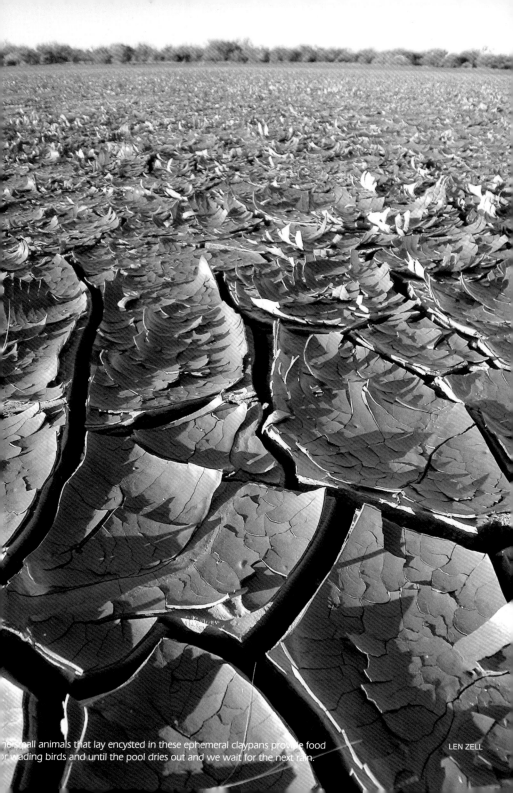

The small animals that lay encysted in these ephemeral claypans provide food for wading birds and until the pool dries out and we wait for the next rain.

LEN ZELL

Exploring the Ningaloo Reef, Muiron Islands and Cape Range World Heritage Area

LEN ZELL

Wreckage of the *Korean Star* is a stark reminder of the power of this coast. Cape Cuvier.

Ningaloo Reef is a veneer of coral, less than 10,000 years old grown over older fossil reefs that grew during times of submersion in the four interglacial periods during the last 500,000 years. It is primarily calcium carbonate from the corals, algae and shells that form it. There may be some areas where non-limestone rocks have been washed onto and also form part of the reef. The shapes of the reef we see today can be attributed both to the fossil reefs underneath and the growth and erosion since the last re-submersion.

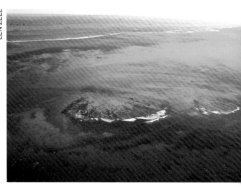

LEN ZELL

Shallow lagoons separate the Ningaloo Reef from the coast.

This fringing, sometimes barrier reef extends some 300km from Red Bluff in the south around the Muiron Islands and around the Cape to Bundegi Reef in the Exmouth Gulf. It is one of the longest and best developed nearshore reefs in the world (WHAN 2010). It has a lagoon between it and the coast that varies in width from 200m to 7km so it can be called both a fringing and barrier reef. The lagoonal floors are rich in life as the tidal currents and overflow of the waves across the reef flush the areas keeping them silt free and nutrient rich. As the rainfall for the area is so low, it has allowed this rich reef to form so close to the coast.

Oceanic currents from Indonesia and the Leeuwin Current bring larvae and nutrients with warm water allowing reef developments as far south as the Houtmann Abrolhos Islands, with some species (not reef building) around Rottnest Island off Perth. Ashmore and Cartier Reefs at 12°S, Scott and Seringapatam Reefs at 14°S, and the Rowley Shoals (three continental shelf atolls – Mermaid, Clerke and Imperiuse Reefs) 15-17°S provide a series of reef stepping stones for the southward movement of species as well. Ningaloo supports more than 300 species of coral, 1,000 species of fish and countless other species not yet studied to quote a number. Three species of sea turtles nest regularly (Green, Loggerhead and Hawksbill) on the coast . Flatbacks rarely nest in the area, as their rookeries tend to be further north. Hawksbill Turtles also use the region as an important resting and feeding area. Eight whale and dolphin species regularly visit the coast with twelve others having been recorded. Dugong graze in the lagoon with a population of about 1000 inhabiting Exmouth Gulf.

Reef walking

Reef walking is possible on many of the Shark Bay, Ningaloo Reef and island-fringing reefs at low tide. Reef tops are usually very robust systems if you watch where you put your feet and avoid the fragiles. Every surface is rich in life but be observant as much of this life is brown or sand-coloured so it is not seen without careful examination. Wherever you put your foot you will kill things, even on what looks like the sand or surfaces covered in apparently 'dead' algae. To get the most from your walk, observe a few simple precautions.

Take your Shark Bay Ningaloo kit and book, plan your walk to coincide with a falling tide and be very aware of the returning tide time, avoid touching things because many animals can kill or sting, or your sunscreen can kill them. If you take a reef walking stick, they are great for balance but not for poking animals! Take a mask, viewing bucket or other device. Keep your camera on a very short strap so you don't dunk it as you bend over. Take plenty of film or data storage, and extra batteries. A small towel allows you to remove splashes or dry your hands before using the camera. If you turn a rock over you will kill some animals, so always return it to how you found it, otherwise you will kill a lot more.

Irregular low tides allow reef walking on Ningaloo Reef.

The Point Quobba blowholes exhibit awesome power in most sea conditions.

LEN ZELL

* Point Quobba, the southern boundary of the Ningaloo Coast World Heritage Area about 75km to the north of Carnarvon has spectacular blowholes – when the sea conditions are right – with water being blasted up to 20m into the air with each wave. These are formed by the softer surface rocks being eroded away whilst the slower harder under rocks take longer to erode and any fissures through the harder rocks develop into sea caves, blowholes or surging cauldrons in many cases. Note the animals which are able to survive on the rocks in the spray plume areas. These molluscs usually are found just above the high tide mark on rocky shores in the spray zone.

Offshore and running to the south of Point Quobba is the Geographe Channel (Baudin after his ship *Geographe*) which is bounded to the west by a rich coral reef growth over an old rock surface below. This is the southern end of the Ningaloo Reef proper. There are many corals to be found on rocks further south but not reef forming. It is a great place to visit just for the beach with surfing, swimming and snorkelling and in the seasons – whale and turtle watching. It is from here that a limestone shelf is exposed and runs to the north as the coast. Coastal dunes and sand ridges come almost to the coast.

* Periodic windmills along this area between the dunes and the sea indicate water under the sand and it normally flows out to sea from rain inland. This percolating fresh water would also have an effect on the erosional rates of the different rock strata.

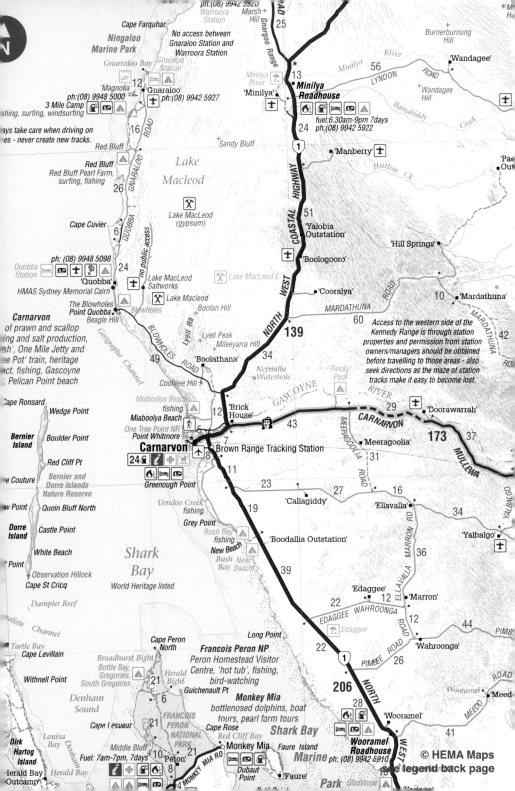

Point Quobba lighthouse stands proud   LEN ZELL
of the sand dunes.

Occasional windmills along the Ningaloo   LEN ZELL
Coast show the presence of aquifers below.

* Watch as you drive this piece of road for the boulders thrown up by the waves. They are perched all along here and they give some idea of the waves that must hit here from time to time. Consider sitting here when a tsunami hits and its effects on everything!

Rocks sitting proud of the surface are great places for the little reptiles warm up in the sun – keep a good eye out for them.

It is very important to keep to the tracks here, as this is a very fragile system where tracks will persist for a long time. The dunes, the vegetation, severe wave washed small cliffs, perched wave dropped rocks, the wave cut platforms with their differential rates of erosion and the whole power of the area makes this a very special place.

The sand we see is sitting on top of limestone rock underneath – where the road has been built you can see what rocks lie below.

Memorials to the dead fishermen along this coast are a constant sobering reminder as to why you should heed the warnings about the danger of the sea with its king waves here.

WARNING – all along this coast there are KING WAVES that unpredictably hit and wash all off the rocks.

* Cape Cuvier (Baudin after his zoologist Georges Cuvier) is a gypsum and salt loading facility so there are road trains, road rules and closures, a jetty, buoys, lines in the water and more action - so beware all here. The 100m or so cliffs give a fabulous view out to sea and down to the wreck of the *Korean Star,* a 30,000 tonne salt freighter. While waiting offshore to be loaded she was blown inshore and wrecked here, breaking into 2 during cyclone Herbie in May 1988. Large rusting pieces of the wreck and some wreckage on the shore can be seen.

* 3 Mile Camp and Red Bluff rate as some of the better surf beaches anywhere whilst further north Gnarraloo Bay has a nice beach and small anchorage for fine weather. Gnaraloo, a working pastoral station and wilderness tourism business adjacent to the Ningaloo Marine Park, 150km north of Carnarvon is famous for its stunning coastline, wildlife and fishing. Legendary for its waves and wind. Swim, snorkel or dive on the Ningaloo Reef, walk and explore the area, then relax to watch the passing whales and some of the best sunsets in the world. There is good reef here for exploration and it is a popular fishing spot for those who know about it.

* Warroora Station (pronounced Warra) is a family run sheep and cattle station adjacent to the famous Ningaloo Reef coastline, offering eco-friendly wilderness beach camping, authentic Station Stay Accommodation

or wilderness camping on white sandy beaches that you have only ever seen in photos and movies. 14 Mile, The Lagoon, Black Moon Cliff, Elle's Beach and Steven's Surf Break are all camping areas on Warroora Station. As with other facilities on this coast marine life experiences are superb. Great reef snorkelling experiences can be had here.

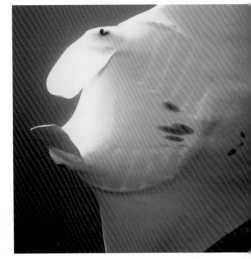

Lucky snorkellers may have the thrill of a visit by the harmless giant manta ray.

LEN ZELL

Whale Watching Guidelines DEC - Western Australia

LEN ZELL

- Only approach a whale or pod from a direction parallel or 300m ahead and let them come to you.

- Do not split a group.

- Within 300m move the vessel at a consistently slow, no-wake speed.

- Stop engines slowly – fast stops frighten the whales.

- 100m is the closest any vessel can come to a whale unless it is a research vessel clearly marked with 'research' signs.

- If whales do come close to your vessel put the engines in neutral and do not re-engage the propellers until the whales have moved off.

- It is prohibited to swim with the whales.

Ningaloo Coast World Heritage Area

Ningaloo Coast World Heritage Area (NCWHA) was declared in 2011. (See Map opposite.) It is unique because of its proximity to the coast and access to the great diversity of marine life found here. Supporting over 500 species of fish – a mixture of tropical and temperate species, 217 species of coral (from WA's 318 in 70 Genera), about 600 species of mollusc and an as yet unknown number of other animals and plants it is one of the few places in the world where the predictable annual return of the Whale Shark, has developed a tourist industry. Dugongs, turtles, manta-rays, dolphins and Humpback Whales can also be added to the equation of a rich and important marine system. With a poorly known Aboriginal history, a sometimes chaotic recent human history there is a growing need for increased management and conservation.

The Ningaloo Marine Park within the NCWHA is divided into zones allowing conflicting activities to be separated and for the conservation of special resources. Sanctuary or 'no take'zones (replenishment zones to provide stock, especially fish) are areas which ensure resources in the recreation and general use zones. Know which zone you are in before you undertake any fishing or collecting. All zonation maps and information are available at all DEC offices and on the Internet .

Ningaloo is apparently derived from an Aboriginal word meaning promontory or nose – the Cape Range Peninsula.

The reef is part fringing, attached to the shore maybe with a small shallow lagoon, and part barrier, separated from the shore by a larger lagoon with depths from 2-12m. Out on the seaward edge of the reef the full force of the Indian Ocean waves can be felt and the reef front slopes away to about 30m and then the continental slope slowly falls to 1000m up to 40km offshore.

To better understand this reef system we need to look at its history. When conditions on the shelf were first right for coral growth, probably about 500,000 years ago, corals settled onto the substrate and their dead skeletons would have begun to form reefs. These grew upwards to about average low tide level with rising seas and were shaped by waves and currents. This creates a flat topped system which can be from a few metres to several kilometres across. Due to several ice ages, (four in the last 500,000 years) , this whole coastal reef system would have been exposed and dry during each low sea stand. If you visit Windjana Gorge in the Kimberley you can see a coral reef like this sitting high and dry. During these dry times the freshwater erosion created many features and shapes we still see underwater today. The last ice age ended about 18,000 years ago and the sea gradually rose reaching the present level about 8,000 years ago. It bounced higher than that – 2m 5000 years ago, 1.5m 3000 years ago and 75cm about 800 years ago creating surges of coral reef growth. As the sea dropped each time there was an excess of reef above the average low tide height eroded and produced a lot of sand and rubble which now form some of the beach ridges along the shores.

If you are diving or snorkelling watch out for smooth limestone surfaces exposed in the lagoon floors or parts of the reef, especially in the passages. These areas are exposures of the fossil systems dating back to more than 100,000 years ago – the Pleistocene period.

If there were no tide changes one can imagine that the reef would be one long solid system. As the waves and tidal changes hit the reef front, water is 'pumped' over the reef and into the lagoons and has to have an escape channel. This causes or maintains

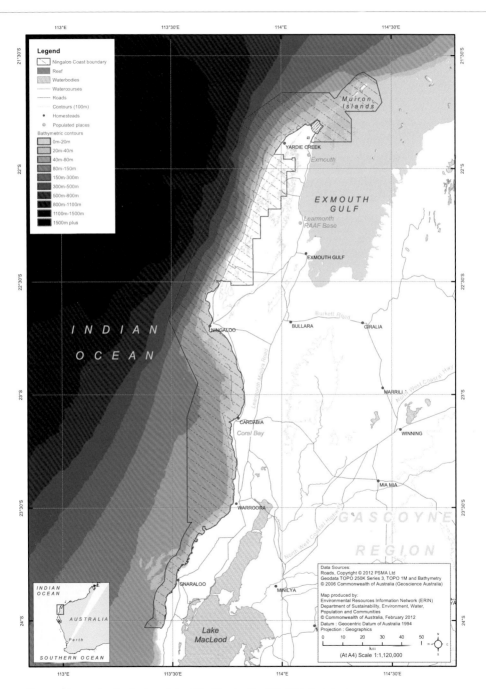

Topographic map showing the boundaries of the Ningaloo Coast World Heritage Area

the formation of many openings in the outer reef edge giving us navigable passages and sometimes strong currents as the waters move in and out. Add the complication of the tides and currents along the shelf and we can see why it is a complex current system. It is the southwards flowing warm Leeuwin Current carrying coral, fish and other larvae that allow this reef system to develop further south than is normal.

Whale Sharks, manta rays and some whales feed on the spawn and the creatures feeding on it. Animals which feed on the coral larvae include the larvae of other bottom-dwelling animals like crabs, shrimps, fish, worms and many adults of the animals with small planktonic forms which begin their life reliant on the coral spawning event. By releasing all their gametes around the same time it creates a food source too big for any of the predators allowing more to survive. The stimuli for this synchronised spawning appear to be day length, water temperature and tide height linked to the moon phase.

The resultant surviving larvae, from coral spawning, swim to the bottom and settle onto suitable substrate before growing into a single polyp. Asexual reproduction then takes over

Coral spawning, growth and slicks

LEN ZELL

It is suggested that the northward flowing Ningaloo Current, operating inshore of the southward flowing Leeuwin Current, off the edge of the continental shelf, is the driving force for the April coral spawning event that occurs on this coast. On the east coast of Australia and the Great Barrier Reef the spawning occurs in November or December about a week after the full moon.

Staghorn corals are the fatest growing species. Each lump on the surface is an animal in the colony.

In contrast, coral spawning on Ningaloo Reef starts about a week after the March and or April full moons. Simultaneously myriads of other animals spawn creating a massive "bloom" of microscopic gametes and larvae in the water. It is like an underwater, upside down snowstorm as the gametes float gently to the surface. Upon release from the parent animals the gametes intermix, fertilisation occurs and planulae larvae are formed. It is their presence that forms the bloom – not to be mistaken for the blooms filamentous cyanobacteria called Trichodesmium. The impressive blooms form brown, green or white slicks with a strong pungent smell while the animal blooms form pink to brown slicks with a more fishy smell – both forms have often been reported as oil spills. They appear as frothy to slimy masses sometimes being a centimetre or so thick often washing onto beaches forming a stinking rotting slime. The plant blooms are also increased by the addition of nutrients from coastal runoff, sometimes forming slicks hundreds of kilometres long.

Whale Sharks, manta rays and some whales feed on the spawn and the creatures feeding on it. Animals which feed on the coral larvae include the larvae of other bottom-dwelling animals like crabs, shrimps, fish, worms and many adults of the animals with small planktonic forms which begin their life reliant on the coral spawning event. By releasing all their gametes around the same time it creates a food source too big for any of the predators allowing more to survive. The stimuli for this synchronised spawning appear to be day length, water temperature and tide height linked to the moon phase.

The resultant surviving larvae, from coral spawning, swim to the bottom and settle onto suitable substrate before growing into a single polyp. Asexual reproduction then takes over as each polyp buds, first into two, then four, eight, sixteen and so on until a new colony is formed and the cycle recommences.

Each species of coral is usually a colony (some corals are a single animal) made up of thousands of individual polyps, each residing in a cup called a calyx, built in the skeleton below. As they grow they regularly pick up their lower tissues and move them outwards with the expanding skeleton. Each species of coral produces a different shape by arranging the crystals differently into beautiful white limestone skeletons which can only be seen when the polyps die and rot off their "rubbish dump". These rubbish dumps make up the matrix of a coral reef and are the largest structures formed by organisms on the planet.

as each polyp buds, first into two, then four, eight, sixteen and so on until a new colony is formed and the cycle recommences.

Each species of coral is usually a colony (some corals are a single animal) made up of thousands of individual polyps, each residing in a cup called a calyx, built in the skeleton below. As they grow they regularly pick up their lower tissues and move them outwards with

Whale Sharks

Whale Sharks are members of a primitive shark family including wobbegongs. They can grow to 18m in length and weigh more than 20 tonnes. The most commonly seen are from 10-12m in length and weigh about 11 tonnes with mouths about 1-1.2m wide. Although their mouths are lined with thousands of tiny teeth they are completely

LEN ZELL

harmless to humans as they feed exclusively on small animal life called zooplankton. Aggregations of zooplankton, such as the mass coral spawning events in the Ningaloo region in April or May bring the sharks in to feed. They capture food on their gills which act like small mesh filters. They give birth to live young and one harpooned off Japan had 300 eggs and some live pups which survived in an aquarium for about six months. Very little else is known of their biology or movements.

The abandoned light tower and lighthouse keeper's cottages at Point Cloates.   LEN ZELL

the expanding skeleton. Each species of coral produces a different shape by arranging the crystals differently into beautiful white limestone skeletons which can only be seen when the polyps die and rot off their "rubbish dump". These rubbish dumps make up the matrix of a coral reef and are the largest structures formed by organisms on the planet.

* Coral Bay with its 120 residents, as we know it today, was originally called Bill's Bay until the hotel was built in 1968 and its name, the Coral Bay Hotel, changed everything! The bay is still called Bill's. It can be called the southern gateway to Ningaloo Reef, is just north of the Tropic of Capricorn and is totally reliant on tourism. You can either enjoy the marine life by snorkelling off the many beaches or taking one of the many tour opportunities available, including scenic flights. If snorkelling, do not go into the buoyed channels and watch the currents. There are numerous offshore SCUBA diving sites, as well as the snorkelling sites, and your dive operator will take you to the best available under the prevailing conditions.

* Point Maud (after the daughter and schooner *Maud* of John Bateman – the boat landed here in 1884) is the northern edge of a sanctuary zone and offers good beach fishing.

* Maud's Landing (Murlana was Yingarrda Aboriginal pronunciation and their name for the area was Kooloobelloo) has the remains of an old jetty and is of particular interest due to the failed proposals to develop it. This is an area of good beaches, sand dunes and interesting flats behind the dunes. As a small port the bay was instrumental in the establishment of the local grazing industries that used the port for their shipping stock, gold and wool. The town site reserve was declared in 1896 and gazetted in 1915. There were store sheds, wool shed, a tramway and other buildings built but only after 1915. Only the remains of the jetty can be seen today as a series of old pilons.

* Cardabia Homestead on Cardabia Station was known as Kunjayinbi by the Yingarrda people. Cardabia was taken from the creek of the same name given by the Yingarrda probably meaning 'red pool'.

* Point Cloates (Captain Nash on *House of Austria* in 1717 after one of the ship's owners, Baron Cloates) has some potential as an anchorage with a passage out to sea and great reef here. In 1912 whaling started here with up to 1000 per year being taken but closed in 1963. Several early mariners thought it was an island with Capt Pele in the *Prince of Wales* calling it Cloots Island and cartographer Reinecke calling it Doubtful Island in 1801.

The lighthouse and Keeper's Quarters were built in 1910. The light was replaced by an automated one nearby in 1933 and sadly the old facility has been left to go to ruins. If you get up to the buildings – a worthwhile walk or drive if 4WD – spare a thought for the two families

1080 baiting

As part of their Western Shield Conservation program, DEC uses 1080 baiting for foxes at several sites between Coral Bay and North West Cape , from 1st November to 31st March. 1080 is a natural poison and is not a problem for native animals, however it is extremely effective on foxes and domestic animals. It is best to keep dogs on leads on the baited beaches or better still not to take them there, especially during the turtle nesting season. Check with DEC for 1080 baiting locations.

who lived here and operated the light.
* Ningaloo Homestead was the base for the first pastoral lease here established in 1899 by Thomas Carter, an ornithologist. Originally named Point Cloates Station – it was renamed Ningaloo Station in 1913. Jane's Bay and Winderabandi Point are popular camping areas from April to October.

An outlook to the coast from a Cape Range cave.   LEN ZELL

The 1000 tonne Barque *Stefano*, 49m long, with 16 crew came to grief on Black Rocks to the SW of Point Cloates and this story is told in the book *The Wreck of the Barque Stefano off the NW Cape of Australia in 1875* by Gustav Rathe. The 1300 tonnes of coal onboard, from Cardiff, never made it to Hong Kong! Also some of the survivors from the wreck of the *Batavia* on the Houtman Abrolhos Islands in 1629 off the coast, 700km south of here came ashore and hold the dubious title of the first recorded Europeans to have camped overnight on mainland Australia!

* Norwegian Bay about 12km north of Pt Cloates was used as a harbour and whaling station from 1915 to 1957. There is very little remaining of the well-built station to indicate the 40 years of intensive whaling when over 2000 whales were taken off here in the first year. This is a good beach for all uses.

* The southern end of Cape Range National Park, which was declared in 1971 to ensure the protection of the high conservation values of the wonderful karst limestone system, starts approximately 8 kms south of Yardie Creek. Not all the karst system is protected by the Park. Cape Range was formed slowly about 20 million years ago when the sea floor was crumpled into an anticline or fold, lifting the 30 million year old sedimentary sea floor upwards. Today we find fossil bearing limestone eroded into incredible shapes, holes and caves – a karst system with plateaus to 320m. Higher rainfall periods in the past were instrumental in this erosion. Cape Range has an area of 218,500 hectares and the National Park is only 50,581ha. This is all now World Heritage Area.

There are over 700 known caves in the Cape Range system and no-doubt with many more yet to be found. Some are several kilometres long, some a few metres wide and many have low oxygen so beware entering them. The caverns and voids of the Cape means it is, in essence, a totally permeable system where the coastal plains and foothills have saltwater in them affected by the tides whereas the range caves sometimes have standing fresh water. Inside some of these caves with their very stable warm humid microenvironments is a fauna not to be found anywhere else.

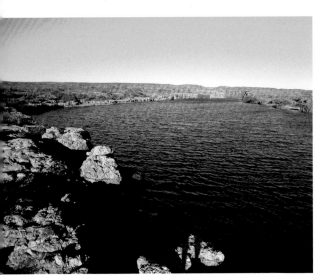
Yardie Creek is a very attractive and enjoyable site.   LEN ZELL

These animals are called troglobites (cave-dwelling) and are more similar to the animals from a wet humid leaf litter on a forest floor millions of years ago or those found in eastern states rainforest floors rather than anything else we see today in these arid lands. So far at least 54 species have been found in this area and they include bugs, woodlice, crickets, cockroaches, millipedes, spiders and pseudoscorpions with the most highly adapted having no eyes or body pigments.

Stygofauna are fish and crustaceans found in the groundwater of the plains and many of these appear to be remnant populations from a time 180 mya when this area was part of the Tethys Sea which was closed about 40 mya, as Gondwana broke up and drifted north. These cave and aquifer faunas are recognized as unique to the world today giving a glimpse to those times eons ago.

This is an arid climate and despite the very small amount of seasonal rainfall we see a rich vertebrate fauna including euros, Red Kangaroos, endangered Black-Footed rock wallabies, goannas and more than 200 species of birds, 7 of which are geographically isolated populations. The invertebrate fauna has some endemic species (not found elsewhere) especially in the caves. These endemic species and races of animals and plants (19 endemic plant species) have developed due to the recent isolation of the peninsula. Over 630 species of plants are found, a high number for an arid area, and is due, in part, to the climatic gradients caused by the influence of the sea and the eastern and western differences across the range. There are 84 reptile species, one endemic and 18 species of terrestrial mollusc, 10 of which are endemic.

Mangroves occur in the park at Yardie Creek and Mangrove Bay and outside on the mid-western, southern and eastern sides of Exmouth Gulf.

There are a variety of graded walks and other facilities available in Cape Range NP – check with the DEC information sources to get the latest. Camping with limited facilities is available in many signposted areas and a fee is payable. Generally here bring your own everything!

There are areas, adjacent to the park, that are on private grazing leases so you need to get their permission to access these. No dogs are allowed anywhere in the park. Also the 1080 baits laid for feral animals will kill them! We find that the best thing to do is to treat the whole area as a national park. Drive slowly and careful at all times by driving at 80km/hr during the day to avoid killing lizards and emus, slowing down to 60km/hr at dawn, dusk and night to avoid killing euros and kangaroos not to mention writing off your car! Always stay on the tracks and note that fires are banned, as is feeding the wildlife.

* Yardie Creek is a spectacular gorge and creek mouth for almost any attribute you wish to name – reef offshore, birds, rock wallabies, geology, plants, mangroves and scenically. No unauthorized motorized vessels are allowed in the creek which is often maintained by

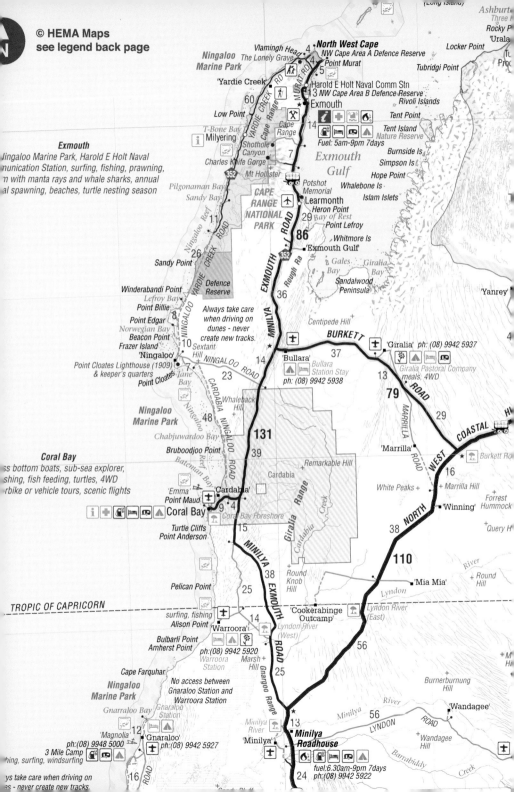

Euros appreciate the Milyering Visitor's Centre shade.   LEN ZELL

Mangrove Creek is a superb example of a relict plant community.   LEN ZELL

a sand bar across the mouth. The spectacular walk along the northern wall improves your view of the eroded layers of limestone that exist in this area. A 4WD is necessary to cross the creek and even then you need to check it carefully to avoid damage and certainly DO NOT attempt it if the tide is in. Sometimes it is impossible to cross especially after cyclonic rains flush the creek open to the sea. The Yardie Creek walk is 500m and 30 minutes return, the Yardie Creek track is 1.5km long and takes about 1.5 hrs return. As you do it, turn around and look back regularly to take in the stunning views.

* Mandu Mandu Creek and Gorge is a great 3km walk taking about 2 hours return from the car park along the gorge rim and back down into the creek and car park.

* Oyster Stacks offers a great snorkel, but enter carefully from the rocks (only when the tide is higher than 1.2 m so you and the coral don't get hurt). Swim over and around the oyster stacks (please don't climb onto them) and exit carefully on the northern side after seeing some great corals and fish. Watch out for sharp oysters when entering and leaving the water. Please do not snorkel here at low tide.

* Turquoise Bay is the most popular beach for swimming and drift-snorkelling in the area and offers the photographer ample opportunities for the classic Ningaloo shots at any time of the day. The deeper part of the bay, out from the shade sails, is a relatively low or no current area. The popular drift-snorkelling area starts about 500m south of the bay, but as the currents are very dangerous only go with an experienced person or licensed operator. Check the signage for information about the rip current. Drift snorkel opportunities exist from south to north here but remember your safety rules and exit at the sandy point on the south side of the bay. Several large coral heads of the brain and kidney coral types provide shelter for fish and are great viewing. NEVER GO SNORKELLING WITHOUT FINS.

* Lakeside has a marked entry point about 800m south of the car park and is ideal for learners and those wanting a more relaxed snorkelling experience. Again the current runs from south to north. You snorkel around an area of reef about 150m wide which extends about 300m out into the lagoon. Exit within 50-100m of your entry point.

* The Milyering Visitor Centre is a rammed earth building in the Cape Range National Park which houses 3D, static and interactive displays, audiovisual showings and a comprehensive library. It is open 10am-4pm and has a public telephone nearby, which only takes phonecards. A small shop supplies soft-drinks, tea and coffee, some food and souvenirs. This is definitely a must do stop so that you can understand the whole complexity of Cape Range and Ningaloo Reef. Be careful you don't frighten the euros out of the shade around the building!

* Mangrove Bay is a sanctuary zone and has a bird hide, overlooking a small lagoon, to allow you to observe the many birds that base their activities here and the summer migratory

species that rest here. There is also a boardwalk to allow you to explore this well developed mangrove system flushed by tidal flows. It is an area where a few mosquitoes hang out so be prepared.

   * Tantabiddi is an area rich in coral heads and bommies and a passage through the reef allowing yachts to enter tracking onto the navigation beacons to the north of the creek entrance, boat ramp and toilets. This is another good snorkelling area, which has year round coral viewing and snorkelling tours in the Tantabiddi Sanctuary. This is also the best place to launch a boat on the west side of the Cape. It is here that the Whale Shark tours depart during the Whale Shark season from March/April through to July. Tantabiddi Creek very rarely flows – it is more like a little lagoon and often blocked off from the sea.

   * Jurabi Coastal Park has several access tracks to the beach, off the Yardie Creek Road leading to rock pools with amazing reef life at low tide and great beach experiences up to Jurabi Point. Many of these beaches are important turtle rookeries for the green turtle, with loggerhead and hawksbill turtles also using this area. If visiting these beaches to view turtles at night time, please observe the Turtle Code of Conduct (see box bit page 54-55). If female turtles are seen resting on these beaches during the day in mating season, please leave them alone.

   * Mauritius Beach (after *Mauritius* under Capt Jacobsz in 1618) is now classified as a clothing optional beach – so for that all over tan ...!!

   * Vlaming Head (Phillip Parker King after Dutch Capt Vlamingh on *Geelvinck* during his survey of the coast as he searched for the lost ship *Ridderschap van Holland* in 1697-8). The Vlamingh Head Lighthouse was built in 1912 and ceased functioning in the 1960s when the communications towers on NW Cape took over the role, with an automatic beacon on one. The lighthouse has since been restored and is periodically turned on to demonstrate the old kerosene

LEN ZELL

Vlamingh Head lighthouse is now a tourist attraction.

PHIL DODD

Vlamingh Head has a caravan park, lookout and great surf.

LEN ZELL

Soft coral fans and whips will be seen by divers who get to the deeper waters off the reef edge.

Mangroves fringe much of the southern and eastern edges of Exmouth Gulf.

TERRY DONE

light system and rotating glass lenses - the only working one left in Australia. The old Lightkeeper's buildings are now part of the Lighthouse Caravan Park. Beside the Lighthouse are the remains, partly wrecked by cyclones and Japanese bombings, of a WWII early warning radar tower. To get to the Lighthouse take the Lighthouse Drive which gives a fabulous panoramic view overlooking the North West Cape beaches, geology, Exmouth and the 13 towers of the joint USA and Australian submarine communications base. Note the limestone terraces as you drive up the hill, indicating periods of higher seastands when these fossil systems were deposited.

* Lighthouse Bay has several beaches and acts as an access to all. There are several excellent dive sites here, in depth from 12 to 30m. These are accessed all year round through the local dive operators. Surfer's Beach (the Dunes) in the bay is so named for, yes you guessed it, its great waves with a reef break for surfing when the Indian Ocean is restless somewhere offshore.

* North West Cape is the extreme tip of the peninsula and marks the spot where the first recorded European visit, by Captain Jacobsz in the ship *Mauritius*, was made in 1618. Phillip Parker King then later named the peninsula North West Cape and Exmouth Gulf after a British naval officer. The area has been an important stopover for pearling luggers in the past and during WWII as a military operations base. As you travel from east to west, or vice versa around the cape, you will notice a significant difference in temperature by an average of 8°C. During summer the cooler western side is definitely the place to be!

* The Harold E Holt Naval Communications Station and the VLF radio antenna fields are restricted access military facilities.

* Point Murat (Baudin after Joachim Murat, who was Napoleon's famous cavalry leader and later King of Naples). It is part of the area once known as Madman's Corner due to the inaccessibility until roads were built. Jack Valli's book *Gascoyne Days* gives numerous accounts of the history of this area and more of the whole region.

* The Navy Pier at Point Murat was built to service the Naval Base and is a restricted use facility primarily important for fuel deliveries to power the Naval Base generators. The limited access diving (through one of the dive operators) under the pier offers safe and spectacular diving to 15m and as a protected site with no fishing, the fish numbers have boomed. This is classed as one of the best pier dives in the world.

* The cattle ship SS *Mildura*, with 400 bullocks on board, was wrecked on the reef edge just off North West Cape in 1907 and its wreck can still be seen from the beach with some coal amongst the beach rubble. It was relatively intact until it was used for bombing practice during WWII. Yardie Homestead was constructed using some of the iron and timber from the wreck.

* On the eastern side of the peninsula, Exmouth Gulf is an important area biologically with large mangrove expanses in several bays and some small islands, and extensive continuous stands right along the eastern shore. The Bay of Rest, Gales Bay and Giralia Bay are the largest bays in the gulf and have extensive tidal flats up to 15km inland and the latter two extensive mangrove fringes. The fishing here offers a good mix of southern more temperate species and tropical species especially over the shoals as the rest of the gulf is generally muddy bottom. The great thing about the Gulf for fishers is that you can fish

here almost regardless of the weather.

From September to the end of November, you may be lucky enough to see Humpback Whales, which rest here with their calves, before heading south. Make sure you are familiar with the whale watching code of conduct (see page 71) if in a boat. Dugongs are generally found in the bottom and eastern side of the Gulf where the seagrass beds grow. These quiet gentle creatures are very shy and often quite elusive, so consider yourself extremely lucky if you see one. Manta rays also congregate in the Gulf around September/October – these graceful animals are often seen feeding on the tide line. For an exciting experience, go on a manta ray/whale watching cruise.

* Bundegi is a great place for a quiet snorkel at any time with great sand flats, small coral heads and bommies and further out in deeper water rich coral growths with about 30 species of coral and many fish. A coral viewing boat and boat ramp add to the experience. It is just south of here that the Ningaloo Marine Park starts and wraps around the Cape and heads south. The Bundegi Sanctuary contains some excellent coral bommies which are a popular shallow dive for some of the dive shops. The small stand of mangroves, in the Bundegi Sanctuary are worth a snorkel at high tide to see the thousands of fish that shelter there. This area also appears to be a black-tip shark nursery in the summer months.

* Exmouth has a varying population of usually about 2500 and was established in 1967 as a support for the development of the Harold E Holt Naval Communications Station built by the Australian and USA Governments. It was the first whole town in Australia built to withstand cyclones. This is the closest harbour a gamefisher can access to get to the edge of the continental shelf in Australia and the prime area for marlin in WA. The 388m communications tower at the Communications Facility, its surrounding towers and support buildings is now somewhat a tourist attraction but is a fully restricted site.

* Exmouth Marina was built in 1997, rebuilt after a cyclone in 1999 and continues to be built around as Exmouth develops. It is used as a port for local charter boats and the trawler fleet working the gulf.

* Shothole Canyon Road leads up into the area extensively surveyed for oil in the 1950s. The remaining shotholes left by the seismologists gave the name to the canyon. The gravel road leads along the creek bed 15km into the picnic area and walking trail. Take the time to explore the limestone exposures throughout the area and colours they bring. It is here you can see interesting layers of old limestone and associated vegetation. Anywhere in these areas make sure you are properly prepared and let others know your planned return times. Not a good place to be during summer temperatures in the 40s!

* Charles Knife Road runs 13km into the range along the ridge lines ending at a walk trail and lookout. It offers spectacular views of the canyon at several lookouts and many great photo opportunities. The karst surfaces are stunning for the photographer as you wander around here but watch the many sinkholes and sharp surfaces. These roads are often closed after significant rain events, so check with the Shire of Exmouth or DEC before going in.

* Wapet Creek (Wapet – Western Australian Petroleum who found oil in Shothole Canyon in the 1950s) is where there are some old landing craft washed in during a cyclone. Stone Fish are common here and appear as an algal covered rock. Spines on their back in the dorsal fin are venomous and penetrate most shoes. An unbelievably painful experience but not lethal!

* Learmonth Airport and Learmonth (after heroic WWII pilot RAAF Wing Commander C C Learmonth who crashed and died near Rottnest Island in 1944). The airport was built during WWII and now operates as a civilian airport, sharing the runway with the close-by active RAAF base. As such photography is not permitted at the airport.

The Muiron Islands are within the 28,616ha   LEN ZELL
Muiron Islands Marine Park and World Heritage Area.

* The Solar Observatory was built by the USA and continues to provide important information on solar activity which can affect communications, weather and other magnetic features of Earth.

* Kailis Fisheries now only operates a fleet of six trawlers in the Gulf, during the prawn season from April to November. The prawns are trawled for at night, with king and tiger prawns being the main part of the catch. Most of the prawns are exported. The trawlers now are based at Exmouth Boat Harbour, and returning to the harbour every morning so the prawns can be trucked to the processing factory at Learmonth. Each catches about 1000 tonnes of prawns each year. Over the last few years the trawlers have been fitted with TED (turtle exclusion device) nets to reduce the by-catch and prevent turtles from getting caught in the nets. The lights of the working trawlers at night are always a fascinating sight.

* Muiron Islands (Baudin after Napoleon's brother-in-law) are two small islands 15km north of North West Cape with great diving and snorkelling around them but not particularly good anchorages. They are part of the Ningaloo Coast World Heritage Area and are managed through the Muiron Islands Marine Management Area. The water shelves away from the shore to about 20m with good soft and hard coral communities. You can camp on the islands (April to October) with permits from DEC, but during the turtle nesting season no overnight camping is allowed. To the west of the islands is deeper water to 100m which is popular for marlin fishers.

Karst Systems - Cape Range

To venture into the Cape Range along Charles Knife Road or Shothole Canyon on the eastern side or by accessing some of the western gorges, such as Yardie Creek, Mandu Mandu and Pilgramunna is a journey into a magnificent karst system. These limestone karst features are clearly visible, as they aren't generally covered by soils, and are very important.

Most people marvel at the amazing scenery and the magnificent limestone geology knowing that underneath lies an amazing system which houses a diverse range of specialised cave and underground water fauna. The Cape Range system and its troglobitic (cave-dwelling) and stygofaunal (underground water fauna) communities are internationally significant and contribute significantly to the values of the Ningaloo Coast World Heritage Area, declared in June 2011.

A karst system forms where there is a gradual dissolution of a limestone substrate over many thousands of years. Limestone is calcium carbonate and not generally soluble in water. Rainwater absorbs carbon dioxide and becomes slightly acidic so it can slowly dissolve the limestone. We do not know if the dissolution of the limestone in this system is recent or reflects a wetter period in the past. It appears that this karstification started soon after the system was uplifted and formed an island about 15 million years ago.

Any cracks existing in the rock will slowly deepen and widen forming sinkholes, caverns and caves. The caves found so far are mostly vertical solution or sinkholes and about 90m deep with poorly developed lateral openings. The limestone of the Cape Range karst system is the remains of old sea floor sediments and fringing coral reefs similar to Ningaloo Reef. To date over 700 caves have been discovered in this system. It appears that many of the caves are filled with water and so their sizes are unknown at this time and from these waters fish and other animals have been seen.

The underground water system has an interesting recharge system. Heavy rains have lead to stories of muddy water being seen in the wells on the plains, of strong flows disappearing into the karst and water flows inside caves and out of ephemeral springs on the plain. This is all points to rapid recharge of the system during periods of heavy rainfall. Each of the rock types has a different permeability and this also affects the recharge and holding capacity of each. It has been reported that tidal movements from the sea have been detected well over a kilometre inland.

Within the system are intriguing communities of subterranean or underground fauna. This weird and fascinating array of animals is grouped into the troglobites, that live in the dry or humid caves, including spiders, harvestmen, millipedes, amphipods, copepods and pseudoscorpions. Stygofauna, which live in the underground water, include blind gudgeons and cave eels, shrimps, ostracods, amphipods and remipedes. Some of the fauna are classed as rare with the possibility of extinction and are registered under the Wildlife Conservation Act. Many of these species are endemic, although there are clear links with the subterranean fauna of Barrow Island karst system 175km north.

The karst system creatures are particularly sensitive to changes in their chemical and physical environments. Urban development and runoff, mining and agriculture all have the potential to destroy this delicately balanced system.

There is a possibility that some "cave ecotourism" may be developed in the future but only if these activities definitely do not impact on the cave ecosystem. In addition there is the possibility that there are more animals, such as the Central Rock-rat, believed to be extinct, which may exist in the Range's caves.

Unfortunately most of the karst system is presently outside the Cape Range National Park and the Ningaloo Coast World Heritage Area. The Magnificent feature of such global significance needs the utmost protection. We hope we don't have another example of "too little too late"!

This canyon exposes one to the layers of limestone and how they have been folded over. If you go on a guided tour often you may see a Megaladon tooth and many other small aspects you would otherwise miss.

LEN ZELL

Exploring the Shark Bay World Heritage Area and Surrounds

Surging seas constantly work the Zuytdorp Cliff

On entering the Gascoyne region, you will to be subjected to some amazing sights, sounds, animals, plants, geology, historical information and features. The vegetation types will change with the soil colours while roadside grasses will indicate if there has been recent rain. The trees will have different flowers, fruits and bark colours so note where bark is loose, observe the leaf colours, shine and shape.

Scalded sand in between trees are common and are great places to stop to discover what does happen in between trees – note tracks, droppings, feathers, nests, scrapings on bark, webs, flowering species, fungi, fruits, on ground remains and animals attracted to each.

LEN ZELL

Processional Caterpillars follow a silken thread laid down by the leader.

While driving try to be "wildlife wise," - keep your eye out for any wildlife crossing the road or low flying birds. Green grass beside a road can indicate recent rain so you need to watch for feeding animals. In some areas driving at night or in the early morning encounters many animals feeding, so slowing down is the best option to avoid killing animals or damaging your car. The water running off the road gives a much wetter area than others nearby and so more grass grows. Road kills sadly can be great way to see wildlife – stop and look at fresher ones and discover the soles of their feet, jaw shapes, teeth types and so on. Have a thought for the individual with the broken windscreen, bent body work or injury resulting from impacts with these animals.

Subtle and dramatic gradations in vegetation and soils occur – watch for both. Ample fuel and rest stops are available along this coast but keep your tank topped up as this will ensure you never run out. Regular fuel stops are a good opportunity to meet some locals and look around – this will also help the servo to be there next time you or friends come by.

Some common animals seen are the processional caterpillars and their fibrous cocoons in the trees. They head out to feed each day in a long line all following the silk thread laid down by the leaders – does the last one eat it? Rabbit burrows are often seen as collapsing warrens, metres across and there will be mosaics of different stages of vegetation growth after fire with various recovery rates. Many kangaroos and wallabies spend the day resting in the shade quite near to roads, while birds nest and roost in trees all around.

If you are here soon after rain look for new shoots on trees and shrubs, observe the different animal behaviours from those that emerge e.g. hear the calls of the burrowing frogs or watch insects and their predators. Check out pools for animal populations, especially the small brine shrimp and snails.

At each opportunity get into the sea water – to cool off but also see the superb marine reef life along this coast – a wetsuit is advisable for warmth. Beware of the tidal currents and plan your activity around them.

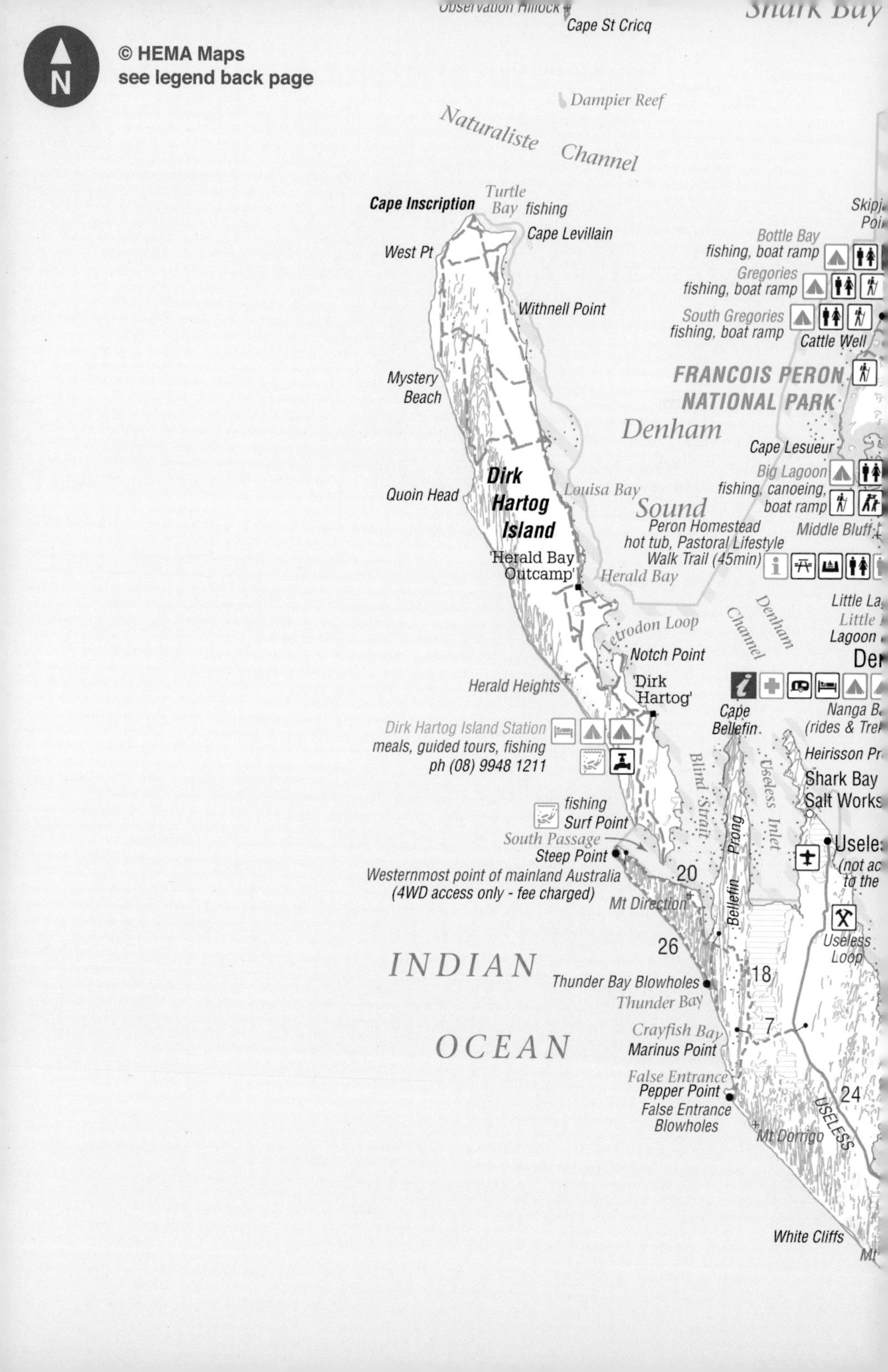

N

Observation Hillock
Cape St Cricq
Shark Bay

Naturaliste Channel

Dampier Reef

Cape Inscription
Turtle Bay fishing
Cape Levillain

West Pt

Skip...
Poi...

Bottle Bay
fishing, boat ramp

Gregories
fishing, boat ramp

Withnell Point

South Gregories
fishing, boat ramp
Cattle Well

Mystery Beach

FRANCOIS PERON
NATIONAL PARK

Denham

Cape Lesueur

Dirk
Hartog
Island

Louisa Bay

Quoin Head

Sound

Big Lagoon
fishing, canoeing,
boat ramp

Middle Bluff

Peron Homestead
hot tub, Pastoral Lifestyle
Walk Trail (45min)

'Herald Bay
Outcamp'

Herald Bay

Little La...
Little...
Lagoon

Tetrodon Loop

Denham Channel

Notch Point

Der

Herald Heights

'Dirk
Hartog'

Cape
Bellefin.

Nanga B...
(rides & Tre...

Dirk Hartog Island Station
meals, guided tours, fishing
ph (08) 9948 1211

Heirisson Pr...

Shark Bay
Salt Works

fishing
Surf Point

South Passage
Steep Point

Westernmost point of mainland Australia
(4WD access only - fee charged)

20

Blind Strait

Bellefin Prong

Useless Inlet

Usele...
(not ac...
to the...

Mt Direction

26

18

Useless
Loop

INDIAN

Thunder Bay Blowholes
Thunder Bay

7

OCEAN

Crayfish Bay
Marinus Point

False Entrance
Pepper Point
False Entrance
Blowholes

24

USELESS

Mt Dorrigo

White Cliffs
Mt

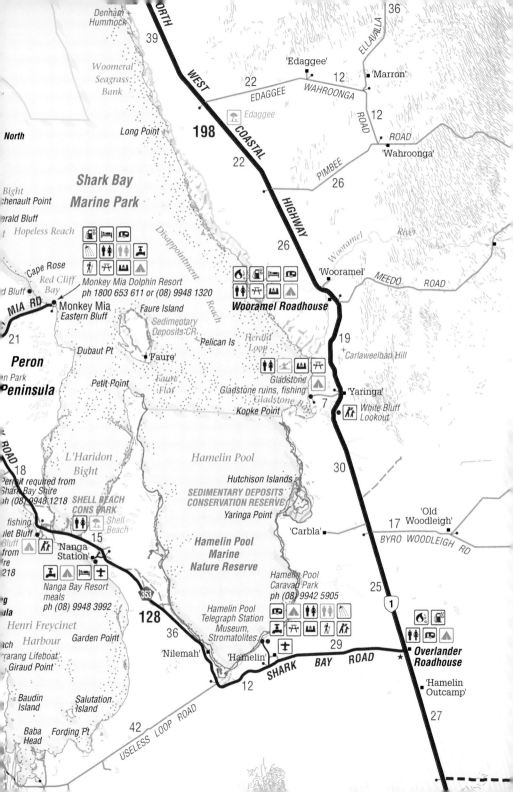

One of the many inlets leading into the Freycinet Reach.   LEN ZELL

Tracks in Edel Land often need 4WD.   LEN ZELL

Salt evaporation ponds produce a massive amount of salt in Useless Inlet.   LEN ZELL

Exploring Shark Bay and Surrounds

* We begin our journey at the Overlander Roadhouse on the North West Coastal Highway by turning west towards Shark Bay, Denham and Steep Point. The road takes us through a diverse landscape with exposures of chalk, limestone, with sandy ridges and flats until we reach the Hamelin Pool turnoff to the Stromatolites and old Telegraph Station.

* Hamelin Pool Stromatolites – see box bit on page 23 to understand these organically produced structures. These are up to 3000 years old but wonderful examples of their 3.5 billion year old ancestors! The walkway and interpretive materials here give a superb insight into these amazing life forms.

Hamelin Pool Telegraph Station is an historic site, privately owned, that houses a museum, tea rooms and office, for the caravan and camping area. It is from the parking area nearby that access to the stromatolites is possible.

Because of the mix of tropical and temperate climates here, we get almost 700 species of wildflowers occurring and the longest flowering season in the state, so keep your eyes peeled for the different species.

* For now we will continue west to the coast at the Zuytdorp Cliffs which rise up to almost 200m above the sea (287m further south) and expose a fabulous shelf of limestone, just above sea level, leading to blow holes and awe inspiring wave action hammering the base of the cliffs. These provide the western boundary of Edel Land which includes the five peninsulas that reach to the north here. Inside Edel Land is Denham Sound with Henri Freycinet Harbour in its south and bounded to the east by the Peron Peninsula. To the east of the Peron Peninsula are Hamelin Pool and L'Haridon Bight.

* We head now for Steep Point which is part of Carrarang Station, owned by the salt mining operations but allowed to be used by tourists and fishers. Stay on the tracks and obey the on-site ranger who wears many hats – Shire Litter Officer, Fisheries Ranger and DEC Ranger. His regular patrols allow better management of the area and maintenance of the toilets and rubbish systems. Find him and the services on www.steeppoint. com.au which includes permit forms, bag limit details and site descriptions.

Access to this area is best with a 4WD, although conventional vehicles can get out to Useless Loop. Entry permits are required for entry to Steep Point and Useless Loop. Travelling the 40km from the Shark Bay bitumen

Warning

All along this coast there are KING WAVES that hit from time to time and wash unwary people off the rocks. In addition some of the cliffs have unstable edges. Check with the locals before venturing into unknown and potentially dangerous areas.

to the Tamala turnoff is a great exposure to the calcareous dunes, salt flats and exposed calcareous rocks with the vegetation communities thereon. The road has many places where you can stop and feel the incredibly sharp surfaces of the eroded rocks found throughout this area – try it with bare feet and spare a moment for those who only knew the area without shoes! These eroded white limestone rock surfaces are known as 'karst' which refers to the formation of caves, fissures and sinkholes through the dissolution of limestone. On parts of the roads and throughout this area the karst surface will often show through as hard sharply eroded white rocks.

* The road now takes you into the dune country, where low tyre pressures and a 4WD are a must. Note the differing vegetation in this sandy country, with many more honeyeaters and insects especially after rain showers. This is a great place for a family holiday that will allow fabulous exposure of the children to great habitats and living in a camp. It is recommended that you check well ahead as the SW winds common from November to April make it uncomfortable.

Several bays to the east are passed in this area and all exhibit rich intertidal plant communities and further out, seagrass beds, with the southern extremity of Freycinet Reach, declared as a Special Purpose Zone to protect these communities. Those who have 4WDs can access the track through to Steep Point but you will need a permit. Make sure you lower your tyre pressures to protect the tracks and ensure safe traction. These are great snorkelling areas especially if you take a close look at the life growing on the seagrass. You may be extremely lucky to see a Dugong.

* Useless Loop and other depressing nearby names were given by Baudin who was obviously most unimpressed with this area for sailing ships and anchorages. It is now a gypsum and salt mining village, of about 200, with entry by permit only and no tourist facilities. This export operation, selling the world's purest grade of table salt and gypsum, has been operating since 1968. The Loop itself is now divided into numerous evaporation ponds to concentrate the salt from the water so it can be scraped up by massive machines and sent by conveyor to Slope Island.

The salt works can be seen in operation from all around here, especially the stores of salt ready for loading onto ships, as a great pyramid, on Slope Island in the Freycinet Reach. There is a causeway that carries the conveyor and road that joins the island to the mainland.

Wedge-tailed Shearwaters still nest under the conveyor belt which was built over the site of their traditional nesting colony. The flats nearby provide food and resting grounds for 30,000 or more migrating wading birds each year – some from as far away as Siberia.

* Useless Inlet has also got a sea wall and two barriers across parts of it, breaking it up into massive ponds to allow the gradual evaporation of seawater for salt farming. These walls act much like the Faure Bar restricting water exchange in Hamelin Pool. The water is partially evaporated in Useless Inlet and then transferred to Useless Loop by a large drain. The causeway you drive over to get to Steep Point has great salt crystals on the saltier (southern) side and you can see how the ponds work by gradual concentration.

The track weaves between and over the dunes so that you eventually reach Steep Point

Overlooking South Passage to Dirk Hartog Island.   LEN ZELL

– the westernmost point of the Australian mainland. It is from near here that some of the best land based game fishing in the world is possible on those days when the sea lets you get close enough. Camping fees apply and fishing licences are required. Beware the rogue waves as there is no safety support out here especially during the strong SW winds from November to April. Several small beaches also occur here allowing fabulous experiences.

* At Steep Point you can stand on the most westerly point of the Australian mainland and gaze over South Passage and the Surf Point Sanctuary Zone to Dirk Hartog Island. This whole section of the coastline extends the Zuytdorp Cliffs type of scenery and breathtaking views. If you can't stand heights stay well back from the edges and be aware that on many days the seas are big enough to break over the cliff tops at Steep Point! Note the old limestone underfoot and see what ancient life forms you may be able to see in them.

On the cliffs look at the lack of trees, dead shrubs and their stark flattened stems, growths of bonsai-like plants indicating what a harsh environment this is. There are many great examples of solution weathering including collapsing caves, sink holes, cracks and crevices leading to blow holes. Little birds, dragons and skinks are seen when you sit and watch, some are burrowing animals and it is great for watching turtles, dolphins, whales (in season) and birds from above. On the dunes look at the patterns from waving plants, insects, ants and other animal tracks.

* The Thunder Bay blowholes provide an exhilarating experience for those willing to make the long 4WD and then short trek down to the vents. The sea state determines the strength of the blowholes, with big seas sending geyser-like jets into the sky. The collapse of parts of the cliff here, show the fragility of these limestone rocks.

* The South Passage between Steep Point on the mainland and the southern end of Dirk Hartog Island is only about 2.5m deep so not too safe for deeper draft vessels. With moving sand bars, reefs and rocks this would be a great place to explore should you be able to beat the currents, waves and other elements nature throws at you around here! There is good diving to be had on the reefs to the north side of the passage and around Monkey Rocks on the south side with about 80 species of hard coral found here.

Dirk Hartog Island, which is an extension of the Zuytdorp Cliffs, at 62,000ha is the largest island in WA, almost 80km long and up to14km wide, with great beaches on the eastern side and some reasonable anchorages in small bays. The island forms the western boundary of Shark Bay and the World Heritage Area (WHA) and is known as a major Loggerhead Turtle nesting site. Snorkelling and diving is great around some spots but you need to explore to find them.

Guano (bird droppings used for fertilizer) was mined here in the mid 1800s. A Lt Helpman and a small garrison were sent to the island to resolve conflicts over illegal mining and he found pearl shell which started that industry here. The station on the island ran up to about 15,000 sheep and now their remaining 100ha freehold area offers accommodation and tours.

* Cape Inscription on the northernmost point of Dirk Hartog Island has an old tramway leading to the top of the sand dunes with a track to the lighthouse, the keeper's cottage and

the post where Dirk Hartog left his inscribed plate in 1616. Also the post, that was left by Captain Vlamingh, was here after he took Hartog's plate with him and replaced it with another. Both posts have been replaced by replicas now! In addition the French explorer Francois de St Allouam arrived and claimed Australia for France here in 1772.

* Egg Island which is about one third of the way up the eastern side of Dirk Hartog Island was an old guano (bird droppings) mine. It may have had an egg shape or was covered in nesting birds and good for egg supplies for sailors. Either way it is still heavily used by birds and the guano is building up again so if you wait around for a few thousand years you may see how it was! Dirk Hartog Island is an important nesting site for Pied Cormorants and the migratory Wedge-tailed Shearwaters.

* Shark Bay (Dampier 1699) WHA – the first WHA declared in Australia and one of only 14 in the world that meets all four WH criteria. The four criteria are: 1. Outstanding example of stages of Earth's evolutionary history – the stromatolites; 2. Significant ongoing biological evolution and processes – the seagrass beds; 3. Unique, rare and superlative phenomena of natural beauty – the Zuytdorp Cliffs, Shell Beach, Peron Peninsula, islands of the bay and the stromatolites; 4. Universal value for science and conservation – the number of species found here and those that are extinct elsewhere.

A Marine Park, Nature Reserves and Sanctuary Zones all indicate the special nature of this place. Some 700 plant species, 7 marine and 37 terrestrial species of mammals, 99 of reptiles, 30 of amphibians, 80 of hard corals, more than 320 of fish, 236 of birds, 232 of decapod crustaceans, at least 16 but maybe up to 30 of barnacles and the greatest number of seagrass species anywhere in the world in one location (12), with Wooramel Bank a stunning example of these beds. At over 103,000ha, it is the world's largest seagrass bed running for 129km along the coast. In some places it is possible to identify at least 9 species of seagrass. The Wooramel Bank is made up almost entirely of sands formed by the precipitation of limestone from the hypersaline waters, due to organic processes and is unique in its size. Some 100 bird species from all habitats live here.

Seagrasses

LEN ZELL

Seagrasses are green flowering plants with a complex root system. They are very different to seaweeds which are simple plants with no flowers or roots, so cannot fix themselves into sand and mud. Seagrasses have a very unusual reproductive process and are some of only a few flowering plants that can survive in salt water. The flowers are very small and the pollen is released as strands. Once the seeds germinate many stay on the parent plant until they are big enough to float off and hook into the substrate to grow. Watch for them washed up on beaches.

The many sunny days help sustain the rich seagrasses of the region.

Seagrasses are incredibly important as a substrate for over 60 species of algae (of the 150 found here) and over 50 species of small animals like diatoms, forams and bryozoans, as well as a food rich refuge for juvenile prawns, fish and crabs.

The surfaces of seagrasses are grazed by many animals thus providing the basis of the local food web and ecosystem and a nursery for many more. Dugong and turtles eat the whole plant preferring the rich rhizomes meandering under the sand. Dead seagrasses rot and are broken down by fungi and bacteria, providing highly nutrient rich food to the bottom of the food chain. Many burrowing species of worms, bivalves and crustaceans also rely on this highly productive community. Some estimates indicate that seagrass is up to six times more productive than a land-based crop of wheat. Older leaves are often covered by a whitish to red coating of coralline algae and when it dies the limestone crystals left make up to 20% of the sediments in the bay.

The slow circulation in the bay, protection from severe weather and low inputs from the rivers all contribute to the success of these massive seagrass areas. The seagrasses in turn capture nutrients, help slow down currents capturing sediments and dampen the effects of swells - all contributing to its success. Seasonal changes, especially temperatures, can have a dramatic effect on seagrass success and as a consequence the biomass of the plants is much lower in the winter months.

Seagrasses can be found from tidal mud and sand flats to as deep as 60m and as far south as Tasmania and this is why Dugong can easily travel along the WA coast especially to the north.

Freshwater runoff can cause major damage but the nutrients it usually brings allow quick regeneration. Grazing by Dugong is the primary natural damage to the seagrass, with grazing turtles and fish, anchors, propellers and effluent runoff from humans also having impacts.

Shark Bay is Australia's largest enclosed marine embayment and has at least 1500 km of coastline containing over 12,000sqkm at an average depth of 9.5m and a maximum of 30m. It is a series of north-south facing peninsulas and islands, which break it up into smaller bays and separate it from the Indian Ocean.

The salinities of the Shark Bay area also add to its unique attributes as they grade from normal seawater of 35parts per thousand of salt (ppt), metahaline areas of 50ppt to the hypersalinity of L'Haridon Bight and Hamelin Pool, of over 65ppt. The tidal range of 1.7m during spring tides and 0.6m at neaps means minimal mixing of the waters. Even the rivers that flow into the bay have little effect due to their intermittency, high evaporation and soakage into the groundwater that occurs before they get to the bay.

This area is the country of the Nganda and Malgana People who with their ancestors have occupied this area for well over 30,000 years. Presently the local Yadgala Aboriginal Corporation is involved in the capture and tagging program for Dugongs in the bay. This is a cooperative project involving DEC, World Heritage, Gordon Reid Foundation, Natural Heritage Trust, Coast and Clean Seas, James Scheerer Research Charters, James Cook and Edith Cowan Universities.

About 60% of WA's prawns come from Shark Bay's 41 trawlers. Their catch is about 1700 tonnes per year of prawns and scallops from 27 of the boats with another 14 catching just scallops. They are closely monitored and work well with Fisheries research and management programs. A cultured pearling operation has been established near Monkey Mia for the rare black pearl.

The area south of Freycinet Estuary contains the unique type of vegetation known as tree heath. There are also at least 51 species endemic to the region and others that are considered new to science found in this vegetation system.

* Heirisson Prong, another long peninsula leading to the NNE here, has an interesting wildlife recovery project there – see box bit below.

Project Eden and the Heirisson Prong Project

LEN ZELL

Project Eden is a project reconstructing and rejuvenating part of our ailing arid-zone ecosystem on the 105,000 ha Peron Peninsula.

This has a 3.4km fence and uses several technologies in addition to the physical barrier to keep cats, dogs and foxes out. 1080 baiting programs continue the work.

Within 200 years, only two thirds of the original mammal species could still be found inhabiting the landscape degraded due to clearing, changes

Project Eden's fence is an interesting mix of technologies to keep the peninsula clear of feral predators.

in fire management systems, grazing and feral animals. The Project aims to restore the ecosystem to some of its former beauty and complexity. DEC drives Project Eden as part of its state-wide Western Shield Conservation Program,

Project Eden began in 1990, with the purchase of the Peron pastoral station by DEC. This ended over 100 years of pastoralism and sheep grazing, with a subsequent change, since 1995 to the control of feral predators, especially foxes, cats, grazers, goats and sheep,

Stage 2 is re-establishing populations of lost species back into the ecosystem, through captive breeding programs and re-introductions, as well as creating a safe haven for their survival. This allows research and better understanding of all Australian arid landscapes and effects of increasing tourism. In addition this area will act as a breeding pool to help the establishment populations elsewhere, as habitats are made safe.

The Project is breeding a number of species on-site at Francois Peron National Park. They include the Bilby, Malleefowl, Mala (Rufous Hare-wallaby), Banded Hare-wallaby and Western Barred Bandicoot. Animals will be sourced from other breeding programs like the Perth Zoological Gardens (Greater Sticknest Rat, Shark Bay Mouse, Chuditch) and Kanyana Wildlife Rehabilitation Centre (Bilbies, Western Barred Bandicoot), and animals from interstate conservation programs.

The *Heirisson Prong Project* (setup by local communities and CSIRO and similar to Project Eden) aims to understand why mammal species have become extinct and to re-establish rare and endangered ones on a peninsula at Shark Bay and eventually on the rest of the mainland. It has 12sqkm fenced off by a 1.8km fence on the tip of

Heirisson Prong. Three species of endangered mammal have been reintroduced as part of this project: the Burrowing Bettong, the Western Barred Bandicoot, and the Greater Sticknest Rat. The survival of all species is critically dependent on the absence of exotic predators, especially cats and foxes.

The use of peninsulas to conserve reintroduced wildlife was pioneered on Heirisson Prong. Such peninsulas provide the opportunity to exclude exotic predators from large areas with greatly reduced costs for fencing. A similar project to these two has been established on Venus Bay Peninsula in South Australia.

Eagle Bluff has a great lookout and camping opportunites.   LEN ZELL

* Goulet Bluff like so many other high points in this area allows you a good view of parts of the bay and is a great short break site with many opportunities for those willing to wander.

* Eagle Bluff, a popular snorkelling and fishing site, was named after the White-bellied Sea-Eagles nesting on Eagle Island, just offshore. It has camping sites at the top near the lookout or down below in a more sheltered area. The lookout has an excellent boardwalk and interpretive display and view over the bay and island which generally has many birds roosting there – take your binoculars. Also keep an eye out for sharks, rays and dolphins as well as Dugong grazing the seagrass beds - especially in the warmer months.

* Nanga Station and resort is based on a large sheep station now providing tourist facilities as well. Note the coquina shell used in the buildings here.

* Denham (after Captain HH Denham surveying Shark Bay in 1858 on the *Herald*) is WA's westernmost town and was originally known as Freshwater Camp. It has a population of around 1200. As a tourist centre it has had a colourful past. During the pearling days the streets were paved with pearl shell and sadly paved over in the 1960s. Note the buildings made from the coquina shell blocks quarried from Shell Beach. Water supplies here come from the desalination of seawater – so don't waste it! The same water system supplies Monkey Mia.

* Little Lagoon is an unusual flooded birrida as it has connections to the sea through a small bending channel. It is a popular windsurfing and walking area, also an important fish and invertebrate nursery area.

* Francois Peron National Park (Baudin after ship's naturalist on *Geographe* – 1801 and 1803) has undulating sandy plains, red sand dunes and cliffs interspersed by gypsum claypans, which are all 'birridas'. It covers over 40,000ha and is managed by DEC, with an access fee payable. The old station homestead is now operated as a visitor centre showing what life was like on a sheep station in the past. It is only a short distance from the main Monkey Mia road, and has good examples of acacia shrubland. Trails follow the story of pastoralism on the peninsula, and the hot tub and waterhole formed from the artesian bore attracts wildlife. Near dusk you will often see honeyeaters, Emus, crested pigeons, birds of prey and goannas. Once past the homestead 4WD is necessary. Be careful on the coastal areas if you walk near any of the cliff edges because they can be very unstable – better still only use the developed walking tracks.

The park is important also for its overlap of vegetation types - southern hakeas and grevilleas overlap here with the northern and western wattle dominated stands.

* Big Lagoon Special Purpose Zone specifically protects the flora and fauna - making this a very important nursery area. It requires a 4WD to get into and then a boat to get around. It has a DEC developed camp site, with fenced off areas and BBQs. Seagrasses often wash up on the beach here and the walks over the nearby dunes provide an insight into what a productive marine system we are near.

Tracks through the Francois Peron National Park cross gypsum rich birridas into the red sands.

* Broadhurst Bight, the western side of the northern peninsula, is another anchorage possibility offshore from the superb red cliffs and camping sites operated by DEC. The Broadhurst Bommies are a popular diving and snorkeling site located some way offshore requiring a boat to access. These are rich mini-reefs with great diversity of corals, fish and other coral reef life.

* South Gregories, Gregories and Bottle Beach are all DEC developed camp sites and well worth a visit to check out the red cliffs and rocky exposures found along here, interspersed with beautiful calm-water beaches.

Little Lagoon is a birrida connected to the sea by a mangrove fringed creek.

* Cape Peron North, the location of the lighthouse, offers panoramic views out into Shark Bay with rich seagrass beds, dolphins and birds . Down at the parking area some great walks lead to spectacular beaches, rocky platforms, coloured sand, wildlife and vegetation for those who take the time.

* The *Gudrun* wreck occurred about 9km north of Cape Peron in 1909. She had a colourful history, where the ship's carpenter attempted to scuttle her by drilling a 4cm hole in the keel when she was down south near Fremantle. Carrying a load of Jarrah from Bunbury to England, she came north. Driven by strong winds and still leaking, the captain headed towards the shelter of Cape Peron North. A gale smashed the rudder, driving her onto the sand flats where she was left to break up. The wreck

Beaches adjacent to the Broadhurst Bight range from sandstone rocky shores to delightful camping beaches.

lies in a sanctuary zone in 6m of water. This is a great dive, fully protected by legislation. It is the most intact wooden shipwreck in WA.

Sandalwood

Sandalwood is an aromatic timber used for wooden curios, especially for incense and joss sticks. It was first shipped from this area in the 1890s. The industry grew to 4,000 tonnes per annum in the late 1900s, but overharvesting put an end to it. Each harvested tree takes 50-90 years to regenerate to harvestable size. Today the industry has re-established itself into a sustainable operation worth about $10million/year. Sandalwood is a shrub or small tree to 8m tall with a trunk up to 32cms in diameter. The Shark Bay sandalwoods are unique in WA. They have the ability to send up many stems from the stump, called coppicing. After harvesting these stems mature within three years. Once harvested, there is no waste, as any wood is valuable.

Partially parasitic, these trees send their roots over to the roots of neighboring trees and small cuplike projections grow on the roots, drawing nutrients from the host tree. Research has shown that some host species are better than others, not only for the sandalwood trees, but also for the surrounding environment and animals that live there.

The fruit of the sandalwood is round and fleshy with a hard internal nut. The fleshy fruit can be eaten raw or dried. Emus love them and remaining nuts are commonly seen in Emu droppings! These droppings also provide a kick start for the growth of new trees. The edible nut is obtained by smashing off the outer covering and eating it raw or roasted.

Herald Bight Beach has been used by fishers for many years and seagrasses accumulate here after rougher weather.   LEN ZELL

* Herald Bight, on the west side of Guichenault Point, is a shallow embayment offering good seagrass beds and anchoring opportunities for shallow draught vessels wanting to explore this part of the Francois Peron National Park. There is an old 1800s pearling and fishing camp here and the ground still sparkles with the discarded pearl shells. Some remains of the old fish factory can be seen.

* Red Bluff is a delightful picnic spot - not really safe for swimming but good for fishing.

* Monkey Mia (after schooner *Monkey* and Aboriginal word *mia* – to rest) began as a pearling settlement, but overfishing pushed it into decline. In the 1960s fishers began hand feeding a group of wild dolphin which have become a major tourist attraction. Due to the numbers of people, inappropriate behaviours and foods being given to the dolphins, DEC took control. The dolphins are now much more in a 'wild state' and voluntarily come in to unscheduled feeds each day. The food they are given is carefully monitored and of special types.

Be prepared for the dolphins to show up late in the day or not at all – in other words no-one knows when! Often the dolphins will come in, but are not fed to ensure

Monkey Mia is a great place to meet dolphins face-to-face or go cruising to see Dugong.   LEN ZELL

Shell Beach is totally made up by cockle shells.   LEN ZELL

Carnarvon is now a rich fruit growing area.   LEN ZELL

there is no pattern to their feeding. Please follow DEC's guidelines for dolphin interactions given to you as you enter the area. This will ensure the best experience for yourself and all others. The Information Centre is well worth an extended visit to better understand the dolphins and Dugong you will see around here.

Around Monkey Mia there is high species diversity and researchers have discovered that it is a great living laboratory with shallow waters, large diverse habitats, proximity to animals – dolphins, dugongs, sharks and other marine species and many birds. There are some fascinating research and tagging programs happening here – ask at the Interpretive Centre.

There is an easy 2km 1.5 hour walk at Monkey Mia that takes in an Aboriginal cave shelter, lookouts over the bay, tidal flats, a bird hide, local soils and vegetation. The trail guide leaflet is available at the Information Centre. It is best to do the walk in the early morning or late afternoon to get best light for photography and bird viewings.

* The Project Eden fence crosses the road as a grid and high animal proof fence running to the coast – east and west. If you get out and walk around here be prepared for some interesting sounds, but don't touch the electrified wires!

* Shell Beach is another bizarre occurrence brought about by the high concentration of salt in the waters of Hamelin Pool and L'Haridon Bight. Here there is a beach of accumulated shells of a small bivalve mollusc called a Cardiid Cockle. This salt resistant species thrives in the high salinity, which causes its predators to die – so millions of shells survive. The shells have been accumulating for over 4000 years and the deposits are at least 10m deep. As a result of freshwater inflows and chemical processes, the shells deeper down become cemented together to form a soft rock called coquina. This has been quarried and used for buildings - examples can be seen in Denham and at Nanga Bay Resort. The quarry building can be seen on the southern end of the beach. A Cardiid Cockle Shell Block Quarry near the Hamelin Pool Telegraph Station has tours available.

* Bernier and Dorre Islands Nature Reserve protect at least five mammal species of the 26 that are endangered. They include the Mala or Rufous Hare Wallaby, Shark Bay Mouse, Banded Hare Wallaby, Burrowing Bettong or Boodie and the Western Barred Bandicoot. Dorre Island was not grazed, so it retains original vegetation and faunal ecologies. Both islands have been separated from the mainland long enough for several bird sub-species to evolve and skink and snake species to have interesting

distributions limited to these islands.

Bernier Island (Baudin after the *Naturaliste*'s astronomer) with cliffs to 45m is an extension of the Zuytdorp cliffs complex with beaches, cliffs and sand dunes. It has some great walks (take plenty of food and water). A bay on the northeastern end called Hospital Bay was the site for male Aboriginal men with infectious diseases, in the early 1900s experiment. The women were sent to Dorre Island at White Beach Landing on the southeastern end. These two islands have very similar geological form and vegetation types.

The Heritage Precinct at Carnarvon is a 'must do' to see the museum pieces and to experience the train ride.

* Carnarvon (British Secretary of State in 1883 – Lord Carnarvon) with a population of about 9000 is only 3.3m above sea level and was first settled in 1876, then gazetted in 1883. Initially it was an important port for agriculture in the region. Wide streets resulted from the use of turning camel trains which were used to transport goods from the depots in town and produce back to the town and port. It is a well equipped centre with wool, salt and an important scallop and prawn trawling fishery.

With the water drawn from the Gascoyne River, from under the sand and deeper aquifers, the Carnarvon river flats have become a major irrigation area, producing bananas, pineapples, mangoes, pawpaws and other tropical fruits. The irrigated area extends 16km along the river flats.

Babbage Island (Sir George Grey after a friend in 1839) splits the mouth of the Gascoyne River into two, at Carnarvon. On your way out to the island watch for birds in the sewage treatment ponds, the inter-dunal and dune systems – great places to explore for vegetation and birds. The McNeill claypans to the southeast of the OTC dish are an important migratory sea-bird feeding and resting area.

OTC and NASA built tracking stations here in 1964 and in 1966 respectively. An overseas communications satellite dish was used to receive Australia's first satellite television broadcast. NASA constructed their tracking station primarily for the Apollo missions. NASA ceased operations and dismantled their equipment in 1974 and the OTC dish ceased operations in 1987 after assisting in tracking Halley's Comet. It is now developing as a tourist attraction.

The One Mile Jetty (only 1493m long!), part of the Heritage Precinct on Babbage Island is well worth the train ride or walk, especially if you are a keen fisher! The associated museum, watertank lookout, train, kiosk and working lighthouse with keeper's cottage are a great focus for the walks and other activities to experience here. The developing HMAS *Sydney* and HSK *Kormoran* interpretive facility record the history of this battle that saw both ships sink in 1941. The pearling fleets that used this area also provided an exciting history with wrecks occurring off Mangrove Point and their multicultural crews adding to the local colour.

The new Piyarli Yardi Aboriginal Heritage and Cultural Centre in Carnarvon aims to revitalise Aboriginal culture and develop their communities, and is expected to be an exemplary centre for the world. It provides a focus for tourism and educational programs within a traditional language village.

Connected to the seas by underground channels LEN ZELL
these mangroves are well inland – Lake McLeod.

The Gascoyne River flows into the sea here although the flow is rarely seen as it tends to be under the sand. River flows are very intermittent and quickly subside into the sand feeding the deeper aquifers and running out into sea by emerging up through the sand. The various landforms around here show several old river mouths probably related to different sea levels and cyclones modifying them. The various jetties, boat channels and fishing and beach opportunities are great.

On the northern side of the river mouth the One Tree Nature Reserve and Anchor Hill Lookout are interesting spots to explore.

* The Bibbawarra Bore 16km to the north of Carnarvon runs hot at 65°C and was drilled to 914m depth, looking for coal in 1905. Keep well clear of the hot water. Miaboolya Beach is another 6km past Bibbawarra Bore and is ideal for fishing off the beach, with some great walks in the coastal dunes and salt flat areas.

* Lake MacLeod (40km wide and 110km long) covers over 225,000ha and its floor lies below sea level. It is an ephemeral samphire flat or evaporite salt lake – smell these places! Especially in spring, the different flowering plants exude a myriad of smells - some are subtle while others are overpowering! Listen for the bird calls. The western edge of the lake, bounded by sand dunes and a cliff on the coast, fills with waters from the westerly running streams and sometimes overflows from the Gascoyne River reach into here.

Old fossil corals are found in the lake, but its surface connection with the sea was closed long ago, although there are sinkholes in the lake through which upwelling seawater supports a mangrove community - one of a few rare inland mangrove sets. The eastern edges of the lake have old beach ridges and tidal flats from an earlier sea level for those who know what they are looking at. Further east are deep sandy soils and to the west of the lake the soils are calcareous brown sands.

Counts of waterbirds have yielded over 30,000 individuals from 25 species here at one time. Note the raptor nests in old wheel rims placed on the poles.

These are great salt pans – stop, get out and check out the salt crystals – amazing patterns, sounds, smell and feel! Check out the causeway, as in places it is made of old coral skeletons known as coral shingle and rubble. Someone has raided an old coral reef from around here!

* On top of one of the large coastal dunes is the Point Quobba Light, to the south of the road to the point. There is an access track to it and a lookout nearby.

Point Quobba – take the time to watch the blowholes, caused by differential rates of erosion, to observe the incredible power of the sea!, Notice the different rock strata and how blowholes develop. notice animals which can survive in spray plume. Here there is also a small, but not well studied coral reef.

Exploring the coast by sea

Every trick of water watching, instrument use and sign reading is necessary for an event-free trip to the more remote areas, especially out in the lee shores and deep water drop-offs near the Zuytdorp Cliffs and to the north of them. Always exercise maximum caution, have ample back-up and ideally travel in tandem. The tides, currents, swell and winds create complicated and often dangerous seas, dirty waters, rips and undercurrents. That's without

LEN ZELL

mention of the enormous sand and seagrass flats, emergent coral reefs and rocks that one can sail over at high tide and not see.

Use of a 4WD and boat combination allows access to most of this coast. You need to have your wits about your 4WD techniques, especially for launching and recovering your boat as the sandy areas are deceptive – use low tyre pressures (10-18psi). The access roads to most of this coast are generally well marked and the locals will guide you or you can use the WA Tide Tables to find them. Some are constructed of concrete, timber or stone.

Ensure you always carry the correct safety and rescue equipment as directed in the WA boating regulations. A copy of the WA Tide Tables (incorporating the Annual Boating Book) is an excellent and cheap investment in terms of the tide charts, best fishing times, safety and other valuable information contained within.

Always follow normal procedures when leaving your destination(s), or a SAR (Search and Rescue) process needs be implemented. Ensure you leave planned destination location and estimated time of return with friends, family or a local rescue group. Also include your boat's name and contact details, especially radio frequencies, and whether you have an EPIRB. Please remember to let those concerned know of your return, so a SAR is not unnecessarily implemented! Do the right thing, then find yourself with a coldie in hand at the local!

There are the dozens of islands dotting this coast. Due to their isolation from predators, many islands, especially the larger ones, are extremely important as bird and turtle-nesting rookeries or remnant populations of plants and animals that are under greater threat on the mainland. So PLEASE treat them as special areas.

If you are using the rocks for fishing or sightseeing on the areas south of the Ningaloo Reef system, always be aware of the rogue wave effects especially off the Zuytdorp Cliffs and to the north, until you are inside the protection of the Ningaloo Reef . In addition there are reflected waves and the very steep cliff-like dropoff just out from the cliffs, which make it complicated for small craft. Tidal runs in and out through the channels, especially in the Ningaloo Reef system, can be dangerous and their effects on the wave actions there are often dramatic. Polarised sunglasses are a great help to see the shallow reef outcrops, seagrass beds and shallow waters.

There are many historic shipwrecks on the Shark Bay-Ningaloo Coast and all are protected under WA and Australian Laws, so please do not interfere with them in any way and under no circumstances remove anything. If you see something that you think may be of importance please advise the WA Maritime Museum on (08) 9431 8444 as they hold responsibility for all wrecks here.

Diving the Shark Bay-Ningaloo Coast

This is an area still, in many ways, in its infancy in diving terms. Many sites are known and many more remain to be found or developed – a great unknown! The proximity of the Ningaloo Reef to the coast means no long boat rides to get to the dive sites – so we hope you enjoy it!

Each of the major centres has dive shops, clubs and operators available. We suggest you only use operators who have membership of professional associations and a commitment to wise environmental use including interaction with the charismatic megafauna found on this coast. When you do dive always follow the codes of practice you learned including diving with a buddy, using a dive flag, plan your dive and dive your plan, watch depths and times, know your emergency and lost diver or buddy procedures and above all – have fun!

Dive sites vary from the world famous Ningaloo Reef and its many sites, to the Muiron

Islands, the Navy Pier at Exmouth, the bommies in Shark Bay, the Mile Long Jetty at Carnarvon, wreck of the *Gudrun* and Broadhurst Bommies and Surf Point in Shark Bay - so the list goes on. All sites are well serviced with quality operators.

Be very aware of the currents and unless you are very experienced we suggest you always dive with an operator. Air fills can be limited in some areas so check well ahead, although as many sites are shallow, snorkelling is a great way to see them. An excellent introductory guide is the book *Dive and Snorkel sites in Western Australia* which briefly covers the areas in this book.

Yachts

The *Western Australian Cruising* guide produced by the Fremantle Sailing Club is an essential on-board text for this area and the whole WA coast. This guide covers all aspects of safety, radio prospects, tides, dangerous marine animals, has excellent indicative maps of coastal features and islands that they have visited, historical information, weather and tidal data, sailing and anchoring directions, local features and so on. The usual cruising 'rules' are best here with the additional preparations for the remoteness, depths, lee shores, tides, temperatures and safety.

Fishing in the Shark Bay - Ningaloo Reef Waters

The diversity of habitats guarantees enormous numbers of fishing opportunities throughout the Ningaloo Reef - Shark Bay region with a few areas near the population centres already overfished. With the collapse of the Pink Snapper population in Shark Bay and strict controls introduced, we hope this is a timely message for all. Pelagic species offshore give great fun and food with great reef fishing near most of the islands and reefs to the north.

This region is so big that you will only get to see small parts of it, so plan on several trips and concentrate on one area at a time. The books *Fishing the West* and *North Australian Fish Finder* has all the clues, all year round fishing hints, launch sites and many GPS points – see the book list.

Fishing charter boats based at each of the ports are by far the easiest way to get around safely and maximise your chances of catching fish, with great local knowledge.

Fishing opportunities include beach, reef, big game and other pelagics. Steep Point has big game fishing off the rocks – but be very afraid of the king waves that kill people here and further north to Point Cuvier. Over 100 species of finfish are targeted by the 42,000 anglers who come to this region each year. The catch is about 350 tonnes per year and it is obvious in many easily accessed areas that stocks are now severely depleted – just ask those guys who used get a good feed close in but now have to go a lot further to get a good feed.

Licences are needed and can be obtained from the Dept of Fisheries, Post Offices and renewed at www.fish.wa.gov.au which also supplies all the other information or links to it that you may require. There are restrictions on gear that can be used, definitions for fishers, areas accessible to fishers, species protected, bag and size limits – so know the rules before you go out. Also know the rules about spearfishing, netting, shell and coral collecting and in Defence waters. Ignorance is not a plausible excuse for doing the wrong thing. Fish sustainably and fish for the future!

Driving tips

- Plan ahead – buy the maps, get the permits (some can take months – although many can be obtained online now), equip yourself fully and plan to have fun with ample rest stops.
- Listen to fm 88.1 everywhere – always great for local information.
- Obey the road rules – they are for your safety and it is easy to lose control in dirt or on strange roads when you are tired.
- Ensure your vehicle, tyres, brakes and suspension are all in good shape before you go – get an expert to check it out.
- Check with the locals before attempting any dirt roads.
- Water crossings should not be attempted unless you have walked it thoroughly or local knowledge says it is OK and only then in a dropping flow situation.
- Always stay on tracks – they are there because it is the best route and it protects you, the car and especially the environment.
- Watch the road shoulders – road trains and traffic can create small drop-offs that are vicious.
- Wildlife is everywhere – always be alert and know the hints – see hints later.
- Plan your day to arrive at your destination with plenty of daylight – this means you don't drive in the wildlife hours and you get to experience the best parts of the day immersed in the place rather than flashing past it.
- Always have the full complement of safety gear for your trip.
- Preferably always carry a second spare and repair gear – especially on the long dirt bits.
- Water and food are essential – 4L/person/day of water is a real minimum.
- Know your abilities and the capabilities of you and your vehicle
- Carry a communications system or stay on well travelled routes.
- If you break down ALWAYS stay with the vehicle until help arrives.
- In dusty conditions stop and let the others get ahead, don't take risks, open the airflow into the car and put the fan on full, this pressurises the interior and keeps the dust out.
- Drive with your lights on at all times.
- If you hit grids too fast it is possible to leave the road and get into trouble on landing
- Grids can be dangerous to cross as the concrete lip can be eroded and knock your tyres and front end around if hit at high speed.
- On dirt roads keep to the wheel tracks and be careful when crossing the loose dirt between the wheel tracks, as it can cause the vehicle to sway alarmingly possibly causing roll-overs if mishandled. This is where speed is very dangerous.
- Add a small dustpan and brush to your car to brush off seeds from clothes or shoes or to brush out floor of car and collect seeds and dispose of them in rubbish – don't sweep them out onto the ground to germinate and grow there as well.
- Carry a telecommunications charge card or a phone card allowing you to call anyone anywhere anytime on anyone's phone.

Road conditions

To attempt to describe road conditions in a book would be suicide! They change daily with rain, road traffic and road works. You are the only one to judge which roads will suit you, your vehicle and passengers – we have seen brand new 4WDs that the owners say they won't take off the bitumen as they aren't well enough prepared and then ordinary sedans belting along heavily corrugated outback tracks with happy people inside! Your familiarity with the different types of roads, your vehicle and your own capabilities will determine what is right for you. If in doubt – go the safe way!

Main Roads WA have an all hours number 1800 013 314 which will give you updates or their web site www.mainroads.wa.gov.au is also excellent. In addition the local shires, police and visitor information centres can help – see their contact details at the back of this book.

Vehicle maintenance

A pre-start check of all tyres, oil, water, battery and general look under the bonnet is essential.

- Check your tyres as often as possible – slow leaks can put you into a spin – literally!
- Do a daily walk around and look underneath – we found doing it after dark with a good torch gave easier, under-body viewing and found loose bolts, broken brackets and shock absorber attachments, wearing bushes etc.
- Keep your windscreen clean at all times – a neoprene stubby cooler is great for removing insects plus a dash of dishwashing detergent and metho in the windscreen washer fluid helps.
- Check your air cleaner daily on dusty roads and have at least one spare on board as they can be hard to get in remote locations when doing a lot of dirt road driving.

4WD Techniques

There are numerous books, videos, training facilities and experts on this subject. Learn before you go – it's too late once you are stuck!

- Walk water crossings before attempting them – and that means along both proposed wheel tracks – it's a great shock to sink to knees or further but more so to hang up the vehicle in the hole.
- Go slow and enjoy the countryside – these are areas where speed does kill.
- Stay on marked or used tracks only and follow the local signage.
- Any sand driving – beach or dune – use 10-18psi in your tyres. Higher pressures destroy the track, can bog you easier and use more fuel.

Driving in the outback

- Respect the landowners or custodial rights. Do not trespass – get permission to enter. Boundaries are usually indicated between leases, Shires and National Parks – but not always.
- Prepare well with maps, local information kits, Automobile Association contact details, insurance and registration document copies, break-down plan, towing agencies for the area and always keep an eye on where you are to be able to advise a towing agency to find you.
- If you drive on and damage a dirt road after rain you could be made to pay for the repairs – check access with local shires.
- Leave gates as you found them – open gates may be to let stock water.

- Stock and wildlife run on grass – help prevent fires – one spark can be disaster so ALWAYS totally kill a fire before going to bed or leaving – coals can re-emerge and start a fire.
- Be careful of wildlife on the roads at any time. An Emu through the windscreen has killed the occupants and they move at all times of the day. Dawn and dusk bring out many grazing animals onto the roadsides.
- Pets will die if they eat the regularly placed 1080 baits throughout the region – leave them at home.
- Stations are not set up as rescue agencies – leave them alone unless you are in dire need.
- Littering is illegal and can kill animals – you brought it in – take it out.
- For cigarette butts carry a film canister for their disposal.
- Ensure you do not chase or distress stock – it can injure them, kill calves, or ruin fences.
- Keep clear of wildlife or stock watering areas as they will stay away while you are there and certainly do not add soap, sunscreen or other chemicals to their water.
- Road trains need special treatment – give them total right of way and do not attempt to pass them in dusty sections.
- For a toilet stop take a small spade and bury it – alternatively take a small tin with you so you can burn your loo paper in it without it blowing away to cause a bushfire.
- If you don't bury faeces they attract flies and there's nothing worse than having flies land on you that may have been visiting someone else's present left previously!!! And you can tell if they have because they leave little brown spots!
- Remember – you may want to come back here someday – be respectful.

Breakdowns

- Stay with your car.
- Use your water sparingly.
- Call your motoring organisation numbers and follow their advice.
- Advise your nominated responsible person of ETA change.
- Rig a shade over car if possible.
- Know where you are – a GPS fix is great.

Be Wildlife Wise

WATCH OUT! – Scan the roadsides, if you see wildlife slow down or stop
BE PATIENT – Give wildlife time to cross and move away from the road
AVOID DRIVING AT NIGHT – Hundreds of kangaroos are about between dawn and dusk, so take extra care
DIP YOUR LIGHTS – If you see wildlife at night, slow right down and turn down the high beam lights to prevent confusion and panic
ENJOY THE JOURNEY – Take time to observe wildlife along the way
COURTESY – Report injured wildlife to CARE(Conservation, Animal rescues, research and education)
WILDLIFE HOTLINE – WA 08 9474 9055

Exploring the Outback Pathways – an introduction

LEN ZELL

To enhance your real Outback experience three self-drive pathways, each with different stories to tell, continue to be developed. The Aboriginal stories of the areas are also being integrated into the Pathways as appropriate sites and information is made available in cooperation with the traditional owners of the land.

GASCOYN**E**
MURCHISO**N**
OUTBACK
PATHWAY**S**

Directional and interpretative signage has been installed by 12 local governments covering 3000km of roads. Some 42 interpretative sites were initially developed and more will continue be implemented. Promotional brochures provide background information, places to stay and points of contact and are available at all Information Centres. The trails are featured in the StreetSmart Series of maps produced by the Department of Land Information.

The Wool Wagon Pathway (1160km – minimum four days) runs from Exmouth (gateway to Ningaloo Reef) through grazing country to Pindar in the grain country. It retraces the steps of the early drovers and wool carriers. You will see some of the oldest granite outcrops in the world, great woolsheds, rural history, constant vegetation changes, lots of wildlife and wildflowers in season.

The Kingsford Smith Mail Run (800km – minimum three days) follows Kingsford Smith's early contracted mail run from Carnarvon to Burringurrah (Mount Augustus) and then further inland where others continued the runs to Meekatharra. On this run see the world's largest monocline rock, spectacular picnic spots and relive history of the European development of the west.

The Miner's Pathway (970km – minimum three days) which does a figure-of-eight taking in the main gold mining centres and associated features of Yalgoo, Mount Magnet, Cue, Payne's Find, Sandstone and Meekatharra. You get to see the oldest surviving and active gold mining town in Western Australia, enormous open-cut mines and lots of history.

These three Outback Pathways complement others like the Golden Pipeline Heritage Trail from Perth to Kalgoorlie and the Golden Quest Discovery Trail from Kalgoorlie to Coolgardie via Laverton.

Each pathway is rich in important Aboriginal sites and culture resulting from more than 30,000 years of their habitation, 150 years of European history and natural features. Most of the primary points of interest have been equipped with parking areas and interpretive signs. The sheets at information centres will bring you up-to-date with these. There are ample station stays, motels, hotels and camping areas to ensure a comfortable trip – book well ahead.

As these areas are remote always plan the trip well and know your fuel and food stops before departure. April to October is the best time to travel these as it is cooler at 20-25ºC rather than the 35-40ºC+ summer temperatures.

Throughout the pathways there are museums, heritage trails and interpretive facilities for your enjoyment and education – don't miss them because without them you have an incomplete experience. The icons without text shown above are located along each pathway to help you stay on track.

The roads vary from 4WD to bitumen and some require enough fuel to travel 600km so plan your trip well. Main Roads on 1800 013 314 or local shires can help with up to date road information – see the contact list at back.

nd dunes are
scent of
il Australia's
t Road.

It is possible to complete all three pathways in 10-11 days. We recommend a minimum of 12.

Wool Wagon Pathway

This self-drive journey which begins in Exmouth is one of the true Outback experiences available in Australia. Take the time to meander these pathways and your enjoyment and understanding will be increased. This is legendary sheep and wool country developed on the efforts of drovers, blade shearers, horsemen, fencers, well sinkers and explorers. Add to that the process of Aboriginal removal from the lands and their cultures and it all starts to come together.

As you leave Exmouth just consider for a moment that you are driving through a limestone environment formed by the old sea floor sediments of 30 million years ago being lifted up and forming the range to your west. Use your imagination here to be underwater on a marine sea floor and think about what this has meant for life then and now. If you look carefully along the range you can see old sea-sculptured terraces – canyons – gullies and erosional features from dry and underwater periods.

The terraces show as steps up the edge of the range and the rock has different shapes, colours, vegetation, slopes, flat tops and speed of erosion compared to the other rocks nearby. When you get to the Shothole Canyon turnoff at about 13km the road runs in through some of these old limestone features – see if you can identify any.

Roadkill is sadly quite common on these trips and can be an interesting way to see wildlife close-up – not something you can normally do. Note the efficiency of removal of the dead animals by the carrion eaters, flies, beetles, goannas and foxes – as most small animals are gone by the afternoons. Often Wedge-tailed Eagles and other carrion eaters will be feeding on them as you approach – slow and look as it is a great way to see these spectacular birds in the wild.

The Kailis Fisheries facility to the east allows you to see aspects of the prawn trawl industry and management of same in process. Soon after Kailis, Charles Knife Canyon road turns to the west with a road running along the ridge line with spectacular views into Cape Range.

A Red Kangaroo killed by a car is one of many road victims in the region.

Stop and look in little creeks on either side of the range and even beaches on west side to see round river-worn stones and a clue to what rock types are being carried down from Cape Range.

The Krait Z Force Memorial to the east remembers the WWII exploits of some very brave men. Along here also note the salt pans and samphire flats behind the dunes to the west. These indicate areas that have been under the sea in the past 5000 years.

Learmonth (or Wapet) Jetty to the east – is great place to see some of the limestone rocks of this area – those used in the jetty construction have been quarried locally. The beachwalking here in this usually calm water beach is fun, with low-tide exposures of coral/algal reef tops and an interesting range of life to be found. Leave shells found for next visitors and the hermit crabs that live in them. Feeding birds on the reef top are usually herons or gulls with an occasional raptor overhead.

Red Gums majestically in water ways.

The Learmonth Solar Observatory is to the east and RAAF base to west. The base was initially built during WWII with some historic gun emplacements around it and was recently upgraded as a staging post for the RAAF. The observatory is located here due to

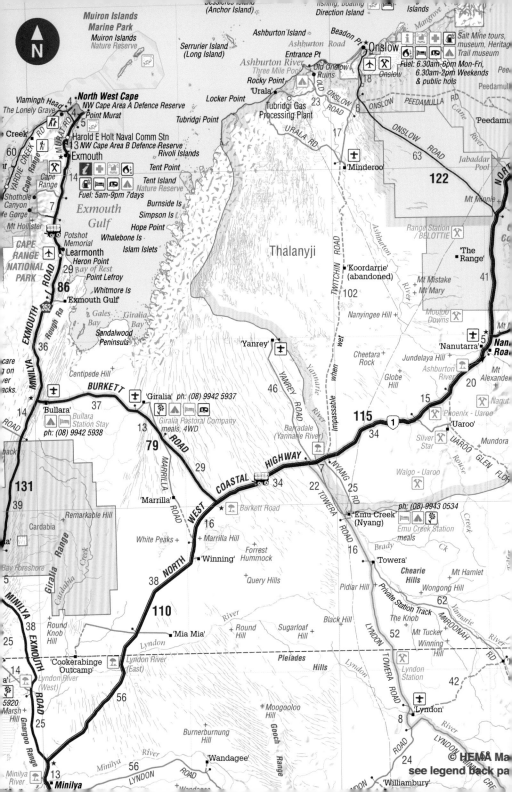

the number of clear skies per year and is operated jointly by IPS Radio and Space Services and the US Air Force.

Learmonth civilian airport, built on flat land that was sea floor in recent times past and soon after we see the first of the sand dunes that will continue in various places for much of our journey to Pindar. Note their camel colour from the high proportion of limestone and lack of iron coating of the grains of sand that have blown into these long linear dunes which are up to 15m high. The dunes are very difficult to photograph because they need to be seen from the air to be fully appreciated.

Rich algae-covered rocks bench out from the beach at Learmonth Jetty.

Each dune is a haven for sliders, the burrowing skinks that leave raised trails all over at night and as with the snakes, geckos, hopping mice, small marsupials and other night animals, we only get to see their tracks. The Thorny Devil and dragon lizards we may see during the day if patient and observant – part of a lizard-fauna making these dunes the richest for lizards anywhere in the world. Dig down a few centimetres and you may discover wet or cool sand – where those critters escape to during the day.

Mounds between the dunes attest to the rich grazing prospects here for the termites. They become more common especially in the flatter areas. Grazing effects by sheep can easily be seen as the distinct boundary between the road verges and the station land as we head into the fenced grazing lands of Exmouth Station.

Mounds indicate rich grazing for the termites who build these earthen homes.

Limestone rock outcrops have been dragged up from under the sand overlay by road works and telephone cable laying . This shows what lies below the surface and how thin the soil is.

* We get a continually-changing landscape as we leave the peninsula and move onto the flatter area at the 'base' or southern end of Exmouth Gulf. The land is lower and dunes of a different structure, as are the soils, and you can imagine that this area has also been subjected to a different sea/land regime in the past. The further south we go the bigger the dunes get, with more spinifex grass and 1m-high shrub area.

One could be forgiven thinking this was taken in Central Australia – Burkett Road.

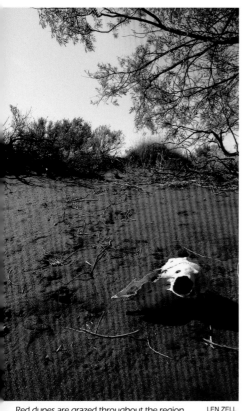

Red dunes are grazed throughout the region.   LEN ZELL

Red soils and River Red Gums are common in   LEN ZELL
creek crossings of the region.

* As you turn off onto Burkett Road note that we are now in the area of more regular creek and floodway crossings at the base of the Exmouth Gulf and here we see small white-barked river gums, shallow creeks and floodways. Imagine this area after very heavy rains associated with a cyclone. The dunes change here, becoming less common and more red as we go east, with a slightly different vegetation cover which is more sparse and less grassy as we enter the floodway areas.

* At Minga (ant in Aboriginal language) Creek white bark trees and creeks are interspersed with 2-3m wattle scrub and grasslands which continue on.

* Just past the Giralia Homestay turnoff is another creek with great white-barked gums which would be a stunning spot if only it had some water! We enter into the red dune system again here and after crossing over several large ones we swing to the SE and run between them until we meet the North Western Coastal Highway.

* Hakeas, which look a little like rough pines or oaks with castanet-like fruit, are now occurring on the dunes. This is a great place to walk for good pictures of the different vegetation and, if you are patient, the little dragon lizards that scurry about and dive into burrows under the spinifex.

* As we turn left onto the North Western Coastal Highway close by is an informative bus shelter display for Exmouth, Cape Range and nearby areas and a pit toilet. We then cross dunes that are anything from a few hundred metres to 2km apart until we turn right onto Towera Road and head SSE. Acacia shrubs, spinifex grass between the dunes and low shrubs are common again.

* Interesting rock outcrops appear off to the east, as does the vegetation, indicating we are now close to the Yannarie River.

* We cross the Dampier to Bunbury natural gas pipeline under the road and soon after turn into Nyang Station. On the road into Nyang Station and woolshed be careful as this track crosses the Yannarie River and like so many other river crossings in the area it can be washed out or full of sand. So a 4WD may be essential or the gate could be locked to prevent people getting into trouble. The gate may also be locked for a few days at a time from April to November during mustering and stock movements. It will pay to phone well ahead to check on (08) 9943 0534. They have four rooms and a bush camp beside the permanent waterhole 100m from the homestead facilities. This is a birdwatcher's paradise. Winter rains in this area may make all the dirt roads impassable

for up to a week after the rains.

The Nyang Woolshed was built in 1912 by the Hooley brothers and is a fine example of an Australian woolshed. There are 100 Black Heart timber stumps which are totally termite resistant and then beveled Jarrah main posts on these stumps supporting an impressive Oregon trussed roof. Originally a 10-stand shed, it was reduced to six and electric drive in more recent times and last saw sheep in 2002. The Black Heart jib pole used for holding the loading boom still stands proudly above the loading dock and can be seen in the photos of old. Inside, the wooden

LEN ZELL

Nyang woolshed is being developed as a small museum and has not been used for shearing for several years.

sorting and classing table, old balance scales and the holes in the floor from the Oregon wool press all could tell a tale or two! This is another shed that is developing as a small museum and the owners have that intention – which is slightly at odds with the ever-present need for more storage in a rural situation!

* Gibber ridges begin near the Nyang homestead as you go south.

* Boulder outcrops and white stones of quartz gibbers all add interest as we continue. Look at how the exposed rock outcrops have been weathered down to provide the rocks spread over the ridges and plains. The vegetation changes here are fun as we go from smaller mixed Acacias to those with buttressed trunks and taller size to about 6m.

Stargazing

During the dry there is good opportunity for some of the best stargazing in the world. To gain maximum benefit, get yourself a pair of binoculars, an introductory text or star chart, a small light with red filter, a deck chair, warm drink and a friend. Give your eyes 10-20 minutes to get used to the dark and go to it. Start at the Southern Cross and then slowly learn a new constellation or two each night. With 88 constellations now agreed on by the International Astronomical Union (in 1930), you have plenty of learning to do! Best fun is working out from the Southern Cross through Centaurus, Lupus into Scorpio and from there around the Zodiac in both directions and it all falls into place. From there it is much easier to start learning about ecliptics, celestial poles, equators and the like. Remember that everything you see is history – the nearest star to us is our Sun and the next is four light years away, so if it blew up today we won't know for another four years!

* For about 25km there is a small wall of white quartz that intermittently appears to the west and well worth a stop and walk over to for photos and to see how it acts as the source rock for the gibber plains.

* About 80km from the Nyang station turnoff there is the turnoff to the Minnie Creek Road with rolling subtle ridges and vegetation changes and then large boulder outcrops of igneous or similar rocks becoming closer to the road with outcrops 100m across. We gradually head into an area of much smaller stones and less dense ground cover by them.

* We enjoy a creek crossing with River Red Gums and sand before a low quartz

A quartz wall runs parallel to the road for about 25km.   LEN ZELL

Outcrops of decomposing granite provide source rock for the surrounding soils.   LEN ZELL

The road cuts a red swathe through the mulga lands.   LEN ZELL

outcrop to the west and small stony flat areas and range a few kilometres to the east.

* The road runs parallel to the Lyndon River for a while with High Range to the east and red-black igneous outcrops, and gibber plains and ridges in between becoming common as we cross the boundary going into the Upper Gascoyne Shire – in amongst granitic outcrops and quartz which generate the stoney white plains.

* Many small creeks run across the road flowing into the Lyndon River – when it rains – with occasional vertical strikes of schist-like rocks leading into ridges of quartz and decomposing granites. Some places have dramatic groups of standing granite rocks looking like graveyards.

* We go over another small creek crossing with Black Range continuing alongside to the west and as you cross the creek, stop and have a look at the view around you here - the pebbly soil coverings, vegetation types and ranges in the distance. It's always changing.

*At Minnie Creek Station turnoff we go back into white stony areas and bare soils with an occasional outcrop of decomposing granite to the west, with mostly rolling low ridges and humpy areas. Wildflowers are spectacular here in spring – fields of yellow daisies and button tops, purple, mauve, pinks, greens and whites and in the spinifex areas there is a higher diversity of flowers.

* Quartz outcrops occur all along here as we begin running parallel to the west of the Lyons River for about 100km, until we cross it about 50km north of Gascoyne Junction and then run to the east of it.

* To the east is the flat-topped Gnalbarrajunga Hill as we see lots of mica shining beside the road, with some quartz outcrops on top of hills and some hillsides are covered by small quartz stones – one hill looks like a white cone. The vegetation changes as we go through different soil types. Acacias, mulla mullas, Parakeelya and Sennas (Cassias) are the most common.

* Near the Mount Sandiman Station turnoff are interesting ridges – watch for one place which is like an enormous 1km-wide amphitheatre. Then we head back into gently-rolling pebble plains until we hit the Minnie Creek south boundary where interesting flat-topped hills to the west and due south can be seen. The 342m Mount Sandiman is about 4km to the east.

* A large flat-topped hill is to the west near the turnoff to Lyons River Homestead to the east. We can now see the northern end of the Kennedy Ranges as low,

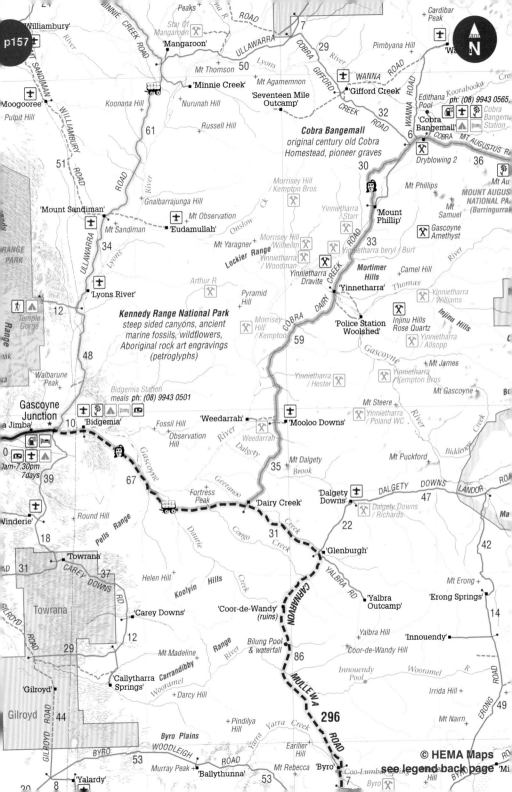

The Kennedy Ranges are a spectacular mesa 75km long. LEN ZELL

flat-topped hills to the southwest.

* At the Kennedy Ranges turnoff we enter red sand dunes for 500m which are part of a complex that runs to the north and south of here, abutting the base of the Kennedy Ranges. Note the different vegetation on them compared to the areas between the dunes. Similar dunes occur on the top of the ranges further in – on the wide flat tops of the sandstone plateau. The road crosses delightful watercourses – with white bark gums and the majesty of the ranges becomes more apparent as you get closer, because they lose their purple hue and we begin to see the white and yellow talus slopes and sandstone ranges.

The Kennedy Ranges are 195km long, up to 25km wide and are called a flat-topped mesa. It is an outstanding geological feature started as sediment filled an ocean basin about 250 million years ago. This sediment was compressed by overlaying sediments forming sandstone and shale. Subsequent uplifts and erosion brought the rocks up so we see fossils at the surface today. All the nearby rocks of the same strata were eroded away leaving this 100m high mesa with spectacularly-eroded canyons and chasms on all sides. The more faulted western side also has a series of springs at its base.

On top of the mesa there are rows of waterless red sand dunes very similar to those we see on the road in and with similar vegetation types. Fortunately the top was not grazed as heavily as the lower areas and so we find habitats much as they may have been prior to cloven-hoofed animals. Much of the range is fairly inaccessible and is yet to be surveyed by scientists. The Aboriginal history of the area is very significant with important meeting sites, stone tool manufacture from the chert rocks found here and ceremonial sites of which we have minimal knowledge.

There are bush camping and interpretive facilities at the base of the eastern side with several walking opportunities on marked trails. Beware dehydration around here. The flat strata tilt to the west slightly and must be spectacular during heavy rainfall periods.

The importance of these areas to Aboriginal people is paramount – the land is their everything and this is a special place in their lives.

Note the shapes, colours, sizes and erosional features of the rocks and overhangs, caves and crevices at the top of slopes of broken rocks. To the SE of the mesa is an extension of similar rock types and remnant-eroded surfaces and a great collection of small hills – the nine sisters or should it be 14 – you count!

* Just north of Gascoyne Junction we cross the Lyons River again and it is a great example of these sand-filled rivers with water under the sand, river gums and sedges. On the eastern side of the crossing is a green metal tower with a solar panel on the top which acts as a river height recorder – you will see several of these in your travels in this area.

* Cobbled roads were used all around this area and were built by men with pick and shovel during the Great Depression years of the 1930s. Go for a walk along the road section and imagine hand-building this so the goods and stock carriers could move through this generally impassable country especially when wet.

* Hacker's Hectare is an interesting challenge in the form of large rocks spread around on the banks of the Gascoyne River asking sculptors to do their best – so bring your tools! Note the riverine vegetation so distinct of these Outback rivers and the effects a flowing river can have on it.

* Gascoyne Junction has about 40 people and is the focus for the annual races and car rally - the Gascoyne Dash. It is the centre for the Shire of Upper Gascoyne, with 439 people, one of the lowest population densities of any Australian shire and houses a small museum in the old Road Board building - the original shire council of the region. Mining, sheep grazing and tourism all play essential parts in the town's viability. It was originally gazetted as Killili (Aboriginal for bulrush) in 1912 and changed to the new name in 1939. It is the junction of stock routes and the Gascoyne and Lyons Rivers.

Hundreds of kilometres of cobbled roads were built around Gascoyne Junction during the Great Depression.

* As we leave the Gascoyne Junction area we go ESE past small flat-top hills to the north and laterite-capped hills south of the road and just after crossing the gas pipeline we see several sand dunes – the northern extremity of a dune complex. Further on another cobbled road crosses the road accompanied by an old telephone line – it is similar to the cobbled road to the north of Gascoyne Junction.

* We run parallel with the Gascoyne River, just to the north of the road here, until we cross Daurie Creek about 45km out.

The Museum in the old Road Board building at Gascoyne Junction is a great local museum.

* Scalded claypans become more common and when dry are red-brown muds with water cracks in them. Small black stones cover the soils further along as the Gascoyne River veers away to our north.

* Fossil sea shells are at a marked site showing 300 million-year-old marine animals. Great examples of the fossils have been laid around near the sign – wet the rock surfaces for the best viewing of the animal fossils therein and please return them for the next visitors. For a biologist to see these rocks forces one into thinking what a rich underwater scene there must

Fossilised animals are worth spending time to study to see how many different types you can find in the rocks.

have been during these prehistoric times and to imagine being underwater in this desert-like landscape challenges our thinking of the origins of this landscape. The bryozoans, brachiopods, crinoids, molluscs, nautiloids and ammonoids seen here are spectacular.

* Sandstones create amphitheatres with some small mesas amongst them as we get further south with small streams like Congo Creek with river gums and washed-out areas due to the intermittency of stream flows events. Geeranoo Creek runs parallel to the north of the road.

* There are great sandstone outcrops for a ways until we get into more quartz country with the small white quartz stones covering the soil.

* As we swing SW at the Glenburgh Road turnoff we go about 10km to where we cross Congo Creek again with the old Congo Well on the western side of the road near the creek. It now has a windmill on it.

* We then travel into a delightful erosional landscape just north of the Murchison Shire Boundary.

* Bilung Pool is a composite area offering several alternatives to enjoy two pools and roadside stops – heading south cross the creek then go for about 500m to find the signed turn into the pool proper about 1km downstream or stay next to the creek and turn east for a beautiful long creek pool experience without the climb down and up to get into the pool here. The elliptical shape of the main pool to the west reflects an erosional structure in the rocks with a magnificent stand of River Red Gums surrounding a permanent pool. Sand abounds and it truly is a little oasis in the desert. Even if you don't climb down to the main pool it is an exciting and beautiful spot to look down into. By standing on the rim of the pool you get an unusual opportunity to see into the crown of the gums – take a few minutes to see what animals and fungi are attacking the leaves and see what animals live amongst them.

It is undoubtedly an area that would have held extreme importance for the Aboriginal people who would have lived and based their foraging and hunting from here.

This is an area where the base rock is eroding slowly up-stream and the pool is created at the base of what would be a spectacular little waterfall during the flash flood situations that occur here. The rocks are conglomerates and sandstones.

As the graziers and their stock moved into this area there were up to 140,000 sheep and 3,000 cattle in a year driven past this area. The pool provided a welcome respite from the hard days on the road.

A composite panorama of the very special Bilung Pool.

LEN ZELL

Hint - Phoning in the bush

Carry a phonecard or phone charge card so you can make calls from any phone.

* After leaving Bilung Pool we find stock route well No 19 which is one of 52 of these we can see throughout the region. Each well had to meet government specifications to water a specific number of stock, usually 3000 sheep or 300 cattle. Later stone tanks and windmills were added to many to ensure a better supply. Where the water was left permanently accessible this also aided the success of other animals like kangaroos in grazing the nearby lands.

* Soon after we are crossing latitude 26ºS and it is signed as such.

* Amazing rock formations appear in the valley to the east of the road with all sorts of erosional features such as caverns, ledges, overhangs and more as we swing to the SSW.

* About 40kms after the Woodleigh Road turnoff to the west is a ridge with a good overlook of local vegetation and nearby low hills and ranges.

Stock Route Well No. 19 is one of the many that kept drovers and travellers alive in the outback.

* The storm damage site selected for interpretation is a great way to see the shape and nature of the different plant species that dominate the landscape around here. Hailstorms of this severity are rare – 60mm diameter – and very destructive – and yet there are many signs in the vegetation and landscape that show us that various events have moulded them. Look for bruised bark, successional stages of growth in the different species, fresh growth from the trunks after fires and so on. All read properly will give you a great insight into the mosaic patterns that occur in this apparently uniform landscape.

* We continue through a wattle-dominated shrub land with sandstone and

Skeletal trees are reminders of a severe hailstorm that smashed the vegetation.

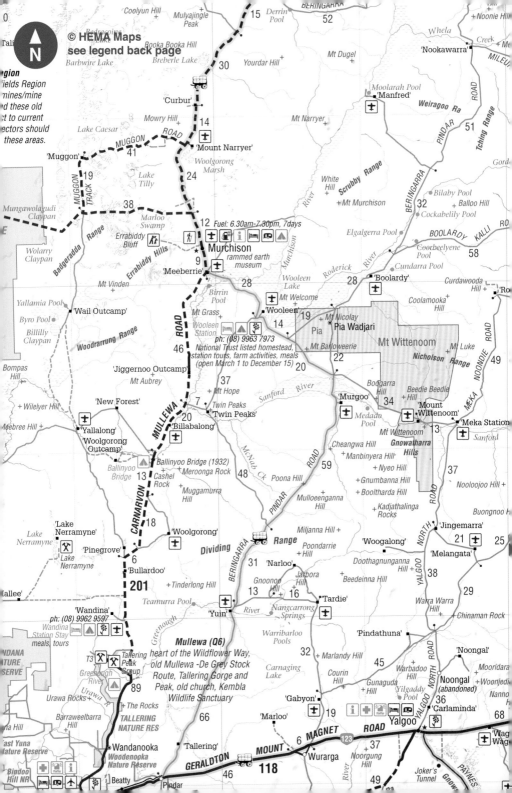

conglomerate outcrops with some caves and other interesting features.

* The Errabiddy Bluff, part of the Errabiddy Ranges, rises abruptly from the plains and is a photographer's challenge and ideal for walking and picnicking. The 100m high sandstone ridges, which are the basis for the rock and vegetation called the Woodrarrung land system, are about 600-million-year-old marine sediments. In the valleys and on the ridge tops are outstanding examples of the tall and elegant Gascoyne Gidgee Wattle found only north of Carnarvon.

Errabiddy Bluff is a real challenge for any photographer with the constantly changing colours as the sun shifts.

* The Errabiddy Outcamp tells the story of one of the many such outlying camps established by the stations to manage their far-flung herds. Prepare to spend a little time here and let the landscape talk to you.

* Murchison Settlement is the administrative hub and the only settlement in the Murchison Shire – the 'Shire without a town'. In the small village there is on offer a museum, excellent arid lands vegetation walk with labelled specimens, and limited facilities. When you visit your presence adds significantly to the local population! Their small local publication *The Murchison Monologue* is informative of life in this area.

Errabiddy Outcamp is a haunting reminder of the isolated lives of our ancestors.

There are two botanical walk opportunities – one is about 50m and near the gazebo between the Council building and the roadhouse – it is just a short walk with seats there. The other is a magnificent display of arid lands and desert flora with identifying signs and white posts or green arrows to direct you on the 300m short walk or 700m longer walk. Both are very enjoyable with a Department of Agriculture monitoring site and many well-labelled species of plants.

In addition the bird life feeding in the trees, especially in the morning or evening and other animal tracks across the trails are fun to guess at who was where, who they

The Murchison Settlement has a superbly labeled walk with the occasional roo and many birds.

were and what they were doing. Kangaroo or wallaby tracks and scats abound. Leaflets on the walks are available at the Museum or Shire office. Please be careful you do not collect nor introduce any new seeds attached to your clothes or shoes into these areas. Anyone

The Murchison River floodplain is flat and salt bush covered.   LEN ZELL

The Murchison River main channel has sedges and River Red Gums to add colour.   LEN ZELL

The 'board' of the Wooleen woolshed is a long walk for those carrying fleeces.   LEN ZELL

who is doing the Outback Pathways should do these walks as they introduce us to the major plants we will see on our drives.

The gazebo has information on local Landcare programs, the issues confronting us here and what can be done to better repair the local lands. The Murchison Museum is one of those local treasures with a wealth of information on local European history, an informative herbarium, as well as an eclectic collection of household and farming equipment, furnishings, photos and the like inside and outside an attractive building. An interesting feature is the reconstruction of the interior of an old home.

* Soon after leaving the settlement we see an area of saltbush plain and white-barked Eucalypts which mark our entry into the Murchison River floodplain letting us understand why the village floods from time to time! Dry claypans and more saltbush occur until we cross the Murchison River which drains over 82,000 km^2 of the mid-west. It reaches about 550km inland onto the Yilgarn Plateau. It is intermittent in flow and for most of the year is a dry and sandy river with some permanent pools. The broad drainage systems on the Yilgarn Plateau merge closer as we go west forming the main channel of the Murchison River we see here. It then meanders through a deep gorge-like valley across an almost-flat landscape. The river mouth is near Kalbarri and is frequently closed by a sand bar.

Most of the lower basin exists in near-pristine condition, with large areas dedicated to national parks. Although there has been little land clearing for agriculture in upper parts of the basin, overgrazing by livestock has contributed to loss of native vegetation and exacerbated erosion problems in many areas, especially nearer waterholes. Once across the river we find the wattle shrublands start again.

* As we continue SE at 28km we find a granite boulder outcrop.

* Keep a good eye out to the east for Mount Welcome, quite a way out, which is cone-shaped and stands at 364m.

* Wooleen Woolshed was built in 1922 and was still in use until it blew down in 2006. It was an old wool press with ballasted gates, that lifted up with ease, without having to be forced against the sheep in the pens, attesting to the ingenuity of the times. Alf Couch's distinctive curved-roof design added an elegance and economy to these structures. The mulga stumps used to support the

floor and build the yards showed the lasting characteristic of this timber. When in the shed area try bending down to pick up a 6kg weight then walking with it from the furthest shearer's stand to the sorting table – tossing it onto the table and then helping do it for 1,200 sheep on a slow day!

This was once steam-driven system – newer diesel and modern stands have been introduced over time. Walking around the remains will give you the smells and feel of many aspects of life in the shed.

* We are running just to the south of the Roderick River which feeds into the Murchison to the NW.

* The Boolardie turnoff goes to east as we shift into the Sanford River catchment with the 428m Mount Barloweerie ahead. These ranges add nice relief to a fairly flat and uniform landscape with more pebble plains here.

* Cockney Bill's Corner gives us a potent reminder of the men who were needed regularly in the life of a drover, wagon driver or traveller. Farriers like Bill ensured that the draught animals had shoes that allowed them to pull the loads through the harder stony country to the north as they took supplies in and wool out.

* We turn south to cross the Sanford River and run SW to the west of Kundun Brook and again suffer the expectation of water as we share a dry landscape.

* The Historic Fence is one of the oldest in the Murchison having been built of mulga and wire around 1880. The manner in which the posts were cut and stayed and the size of the wires, all go to show a fence built to last – and it has – for 125 years!. Few last as well, although termite action may eventually spell the end of this amazing structure. For those interested the grazier, Frank Wittenoom, who had this fence built, has had his biography written – *A Varied and Versatile Life*. It is a good example of the lives, thinking and attitudes of peoples of the day.

This fence is over 125 years old and still solid!

Take a look at the scalded land in between mulga shrubs – what was this country like prior to sheep and rabbits?

If you see carrion eaters at roadkills or snakes, lizards and Emus crossing the road do your best to avoid them. With any animal crossing the road brake carefully and aim behind them rather where they are heading so they move away from your track.

* This is now gold country and you may see test drilling sites. Miners are looking for alluvial gold deposits to depths of about 260m and more may be found in the future – so keep an eye out. If you see an operation in process, keep clear unless invited to visit.

A clear message to keep well away from mines and exploration sites!

Once the site of a small settlement and now home for termite mounds. Bumbinyoo Flats.   LEN ZELL

The old well at Bumbinyoo Flats has fallen into disrepair.   LEN ZELL

* We enter the Greenough River floodplain and several interesting watercourses coming in from the east. Then begins an area of cypress pines on white to yellow sand ridges for a few kilometres and then back into 5m-high mulga and the pines petering out with this change occuring several times along here.

* Small termite mounds to 1m are almost mushroom-shaped here – presumably eroded away at at their bases when pooled water was here in this open-plain area.

* The buildings at the crossroads at Bumbinyoo Flats are now little more than a memory of the life at the point where the east-west Geraldton-to-Cue coach road and the Pindar Murchison north-south wagon route met. The name has been spelt many ways but this does not change the importance of these crossroads in history. Here there was a 'wayside house' from 1892, called the Traveller's Rest, that provided comfort, food and reasonable prices for travellers. Those with stock were very appreciative of the spring and well that provided a reliable water supply; 50m north of the interpretive sign is the old well with remnants of its fence still standing. When the rail came in 1896 Bumbinyoo quickly disappeared. Glass, metal, harness fittings and other debris are still scattered around the whole area.

* We pass through more saltbush-rich claypans in a flat area in a valley just before the Tallering Station station stay, and then into 8-9m-high Eucalypts intermixed with mulga.

* As we pass the Murchison Shire boundary sign we are getting close to the wheat fields near the road and as you approach the township of Pindar you can see the bulk wheat storage facility here. Mulga is getting more dense, associated with better soils and may enjoy a little more rain.

* Pindar is the southern end of the Wool Wagon Pathway and was an important rail head for the teamsters of old. Here for local station owners was the source of feed during drought, supplies all year and a way to get products out to get the cash in to pay for all. The movements of the railhead to the east over the years saw these rail head towns wax and wane and the efficiencies of the stations and mines as well. The closure of the railway in 1978 saw the end of more than a hundred years of service with roads becoming the sole transport system.

Near Bumbinyoo Flats you see the transition
from scalded land into mulga shrublands.

LEN ZELL

Miner's Pathway

An old gold battery reminds us of Yalgoo's past.

Warning

As there are many old mining tunnels and shafts throughout this area always be extremely careful when walking off marked tracks and be especially vigilant with children.

The explorer Robert Austin noted the mineral potential of the Gascoyne and Murchison during his exploration of the regions in 1854. It was 35 years after that when the first prospectors came into the region and as a result another gold rush was on. Thousands came to the area to seek their fortunes.

The Miner's Pathway allows you, limited only by your imagination, to relive the many tales woven around the sites of this region. Take your time and keep your eyes open – you never know your luck!

This is a trip where you will again see subtle and dramatic changes in vegetation from little or none, to 1m high, 2-3m high, 5m and then 6-15m with mostly Acacias and other mulga species – the trick is to be able to observe those changes and try to explain them.

We follow the Miner's Pathway along the route Yalgoo – Payne's Find – Mount Magnet, Then Yalgoo – Mount Magnet – Sandstone – Meekatharra – Cue – Mount Magnet.

Yalgoo to Payne's Find

* Yalgoo, with about 50 people is an historic town and offers a museum of Aboriginal and recent-history artefacts in the old courthouse building with keys available from the Shire Office, General Store or Hotel. Next to the museum are the restored police station and jail, well worth a visit. In 1919 a small chapel was designed by Monsignor John Hawes and built for the Dominican Sisters – it still proudly stands on a small rise. The old railway station was built for the railway to Mullewa in 1898 and closed in 1978. It has been fully restored as the Sporting Complex with fuel, information and toilet facilities.

Five kilometres out of town the old Cue cemetery allows an imaginary glimpse into the trials and tribulations of the early settlers here. It is possible to follow an historical trail starting here, or maybe you'd like to join those who fossick for gold? The area was known as Yalgo by the Aboriginal people long before Europeans arrived. For them it was a sacred area and known as the source of thunder and lightning.

* Joker's Tunnel is 12km SE out of town and is on the start of the Gnows Nest Range running SE adjacent to the road for

LEN ZELL

An old chapel built for the Dominican Sisters has stood in Yalgoo since 1919.

LEN ZELL

Joker's Tunnel shows the tenacity of the old miners digging through solid rock.

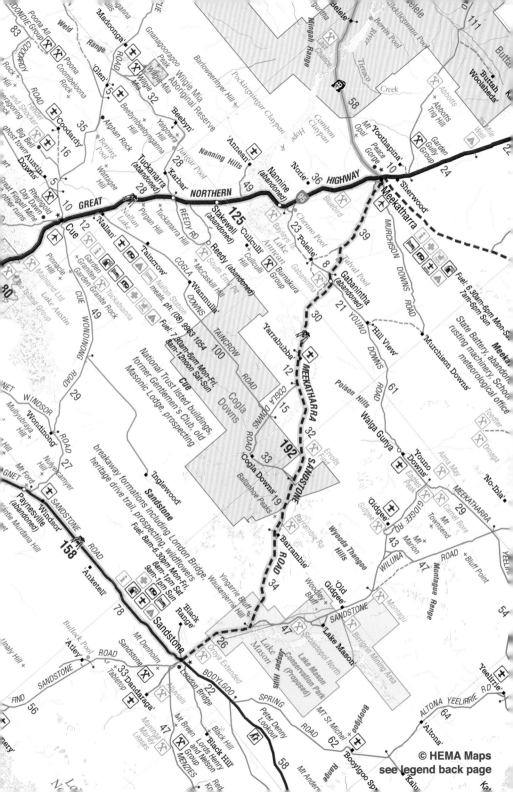

© HEMA Maps
see legend back page

The rocks inside Jokers Tunnel hint at gold nearby.   LEN ZELL

Lake Wownaminya glimmers in the distance after rain.   LEN ZELL

Archways and other eroded features are common on Gnows Nest Range.   LEN ZELL

about 50km. Take a torch and be aware that there are likely to be all sorts of insects, especially crickets and spiders, in there sometimes. There are warnings that snakes could be in there as well! This is an interesting mine that goes from one side of the hill to the other and apparently yielded little, if any gold, so don't get your hopes up! It is a great place to explore the different rock types that occur through the hill. Take your torch and see how many you can find.

It is from the mine's entrance that you will often see interesting fauna and a great view of Lake Wownaminya which lies across the road and Wownaminya Hill at 432m to the east. Be prepared to see small lizards, snakes, goannas, kangaroos, wallabies, Emus and the occasional goat.

* We travel through a gap in the southern end of Gnows Nest Range many interesting eroded faces with small caves and overhangs can be seen. There are mines both sides of the road as we travel, with the Golden Grove Mine being one of the most obvious on the western side. These ranges, water holes and lands were a very important part of the Aboriginal usage of this area, and sadly if there was any art that interests non-Aboriginal people, it is unlikely to have survived on these rock surfaces as they erode quite easily. We find several archways and other great rock shapes – great photos!

Reds, oranges, browns, whites and grey in the local rocks point to an interesting geology.

* Thunderlarra Station Stay is to the west where it appears that goats are farmed in this area. Excellent claypans start appearing on both sides before we travel into an area of tall Eucalypts to 12-15m with rough dark bark, and then it changes back to saltbush country again. We have been traversing the lowlands associated with Mongers Lake, before we get into rougher country with a range of hills and the odd mullock heap indicating exploration and mining here at some time.

* A sad story is told at the cemetery near the Field's Find Gold Mine of four men who died in the search for gold. A large quantity of explosives went off accidentally killing four young men and their pieces were gathered and buried here. The partially-restored and lonely cemetery is another stark reminder of the difficulties and risks of working in this industry. It also provokes thoughts of how many died and were never found, or their resting places never marked.

* The Bullajungadeah Hills surround us as we cross Mongers Lake proper which appears as salt pans in amongst a series of low-peaked, softly-rounded hills with

lots of interesting erosional features and cave-like appearances. The vegetation is primarily mulga in between bare areas covered by quartz rocks about 2cm in diameter and then back into fine black pebbles covering the ground. Once out of the hills we get back into bare clay soils.

Always watch for roos and wallabies in this country as they will often come out from their shady rest spots when disturbed at any time of the day, and may hop right across in front of you.

* Old stock route wells, some with a mill and water tank, and old sheep yards on road sides, continue to remind us that this area was travelled by the drovers of old and still supports stock today.

* Note now the patches of tall mulga with grey bark and red polished bark and the changes back to low Acacia shrubs all showing the continuing variations in soil types.

There are a few spots along here where you can stop and see out over a relatively large area – stop, and have a look to see if you can pick up those zones of different vegetation.

* Payne's Find has the oldest-operating gold battery in the state, a hotel, an excellent museum and curio shop covering the pastoral and mining history. The battery is now privately owned and still operates from time to time. This lets one see the process that had many a man stand and watch to see if his efforts were to be rewarded with a bag of gold.

It is here where the southern and northern wildflower provinces overlap leading to an interesting intermixing of species when in bloom.

LEN ZELL

Four miners were in so many pieces after the blast in a mine nearby they buried them together in two coffins.

LEN ZELL

One of the many refurbished wells found on the old stock routes throughout the region.

Payne's Find to Mount Magnet

* As we head north on the Great Northern Highway towards Mount Magnet note the tall mulga trees up to 10m in intermittent patches.

'Mulga' is the name given multi-stemmed Acacia shrubs, primarily a hardy

LEN ZELL

The heavy metal cylinders crush the rock in the old stampers.

Another old well, this one with the windlass system in place, shows that there is always water around.   LEN ZELL

Overlap of the north and south floral provinces mean more species in this area.   LEN ZELL

shrub or small tree from a tuberous and woody rootstock which often dominate grassy, open woodland characteristic of most of the arid to semi-arid parts of Australia.

Bush tucker abounds, especially from the seeds of the mulga and biologically interesting things happen here. Many birds frequent them and it is fun to hear the dawn chorus of honeyeaters who need to get their early-morning feed of nectar and again in the evenings with some chittering and calls that go on all day.

If these deep-rooted mulga plants are removed, the salt-rich water table rises. Any low valley areas become salt-laden as water evaporates out of the surface of soil causing hypersalinity. Some success with lowering the water table has been achieved by planting deep-rooted species in strategic areas.

* You can get occasional vistas overlooking mulga expanses showing that soft blue hue from oils in leaves being given off in the heat. This oil can be explosive on very hot still days should a fire start. Old seismic lines, bores, wells and tracks all indicate the mix of mining and grazing that has occurred here.

* About 90km from Mount Magnet we are adjacent to Canning Hill and to the east we get a good outlook over the uniformity of this country and some low ranges in the distance ahead. Turnoffs for gold mine operations are regular as we get into stands of pines and oak trees with multiple stems

* Kurrajong trees occur regularly amongst patches of fairly clear land with low small Acacias interspersed with grass as we get to the Kirkalocka Station stay with its caravan park and station tours.

* We rise a little in the midst of a series of hills and dales

A composite panorama from the Mount Warramboo Lookout at Mount Magnet..

LEN ZELL

and scalded pebble covered soils with small Acacias and grass which can show dramatic seasonal changes as well. To the east, interesting rock exposures can be seen on a north-south ridge.

* We go in and out of areas of cypress pines, kurrajongs and buttressed dark-leafed trees as the slight changes in elevation and soil types occur on our way into Mount Magnet.

* Mount Magnet is the oldest-operating gold mining town in WA and provides a hub from which to explore the rest of the mining features of this area especially on the 37km circular Tourist Trail. In town the 1.4km Heritage Walk is a great way to relive the history, by visiting the old Post Office, school buildings and many others. The Mining and Pastoral Museum is also a must. By visiting the Mount Warramboo Lookout you get to see the overviews for the town and nearby open-cut mine sites still working. The map available at the Information Centre brings into perspective the size, number and locations of the mines in the area.

Some of the mining operation's names are rather incongruous when one sees their effects! Note the way in which plants are able to invade and survive even in these very rugged conditions. Always be very careful around these mines as the trucks carry up to 80 tonnes and find it hard to stop! This is also an area where gem fossicking is popular.

Yalgoo to Mount Magnet

* To get from Yalgoo to Mount Magnet we go ENE on the Mount Magnet Road for 124km and pass over a small ridge to the north. There are two hills to the south and one to SW, this is part of small range, with shrublands thinning out to sparse vegetation initially as we get into a gibber plain. Then further on termite mounds on the north side of road introduce an area of sandy soil with better cover and Acacias getting bigger and denser. The termite mounds continue on and off with some groups of them being good for pictures. Some dramatic differences in the vegetation can be due to fire effects or soil changes.

* At the Mount Magnet and Yalgoo shire boundary we see the continuation of irregular subtle changes in vegetation, soil colours, texture, covering, flat or sloped, pebbles, rocks, gibbers, stones or outcrops nearby that contribute to the nearby soils and their rock coverings.

* Over the Culgabberoo Flats try comparing each side of the road and work out why each side is so different – fire, soil types, grazing pressure, aspect or what?

* We go through a gap between two small ridges as we come into hillier country associated with Mount Magnet about 12kms to the north. The ridges here are covered with polished gibbers.

* About 5km out of town there is great spot as you approach Mount Magnet to see the size of the mullock heaps indicating the significant mining operations that have been conducted here. Just out of town we pass the power generation plant for Mount Magnet.

* We could almost call all of Mount Magnet a mining interpretive site, with the museum and some parts of town showing the historical and then presently-operational mines. Be extremely careful where you go and supervise children at all times as the big trucks are difficult to stop and the holes in the ground very deep!

Note the changes in the colours of the mullock heaps and you can see that the various layers of the earth yield different colours showing that each is geologically different. Also there are some attempts at rehabilitation going on – some natural and some planned.

The Payneville cemetery has old building materials about one kilometre away.   LEN ZELL

The refurbished historic Post Office at Sandstone.   LEN ZELL

Mount Magnet to Sandstone

* Sandstone is 158km to the east and we see changes in soil types from pebble, stony, and gibber plains and changes in vegetation species and sizes. As you drive through this country side imagine how much gold you could be driving past and above! This is what keeps the gold miners searching – still!

* Just before the Youanmi Road off to south there are quartz outcrops on the southern side of the road and excellent examples of quartz gibbers covering the landscape; this then fades out to be replaced by black shiny pebbles. This is an area of low-rolling hills with a small range due east and continuing both subtle and dramatic changes in vegetation

* The Paynesville Cemetery is a small location and all that remains of a small town that sprung up quickly and just as quickly died away. To the east about a kilometre there are more bits of corrugated iron and other remnants. There are many old mine sites around so be watchful. Should you sit and listen, the whispering voices in the trees tell the tales of times past!

* At the Windsor Homestead turnoff to north you can see (from the road) the woolshed, buildings and some mining buildings from the Windsor Castle Mine.

* About 30km on from the shire boundary we see 8-10m Eucalypts on a ridge top with dark barks, then Hakeas become more common, until we move into low saltbush shrubland and this pattern repeats until we reach Sandstone.

* Sandstone, gazetted in 1906, is a crossroads between the WA coast and Outback inland with a population of about 380. This is the heart of the breakaway country with the rusty sandstone rocks giving its name to the town. Past and present gold mining have contributed to the continuance of the town. Its history can be found in the information centre and excellent library. The

Heritage Trail leads you to each of the points of interest for a combination half day walk/drive trail of 18km.

There are numerous mines about here, mostly abandoned, demonstrating the incredible amount of effort that goes into the search for the elusive gold.

* London Bridge was formed by erosion out of part of a remnant basalt flow about 350-million-years-old and 800m long. This is a fabulous photographic spot and well worth exploration, carefully, of the whole site whilst avoiding ALL climbing.

* The brewery in the breakaway was built in 1907 to service the town's thirst until 1910 when the railway from Mount Magnet came through with a supply of reliable beers. When you visit here imagine the water being pumped to the vats on the top of the ridge and then the brewing process occurring down to the vats in the cool chambers dug into the hillside – it is enough to give you the energy to fight your way through a crowd of thirsty miners for your shout. Apparently the beer here was not good to transport any distance at all!

Sandstone to Meekatharra

* As we head north about 15km out we see another old stock route well before the Meekatharra Road turnoff to the NW and we are skirting the western end of Lake Mason. Emus are likely to cross the road at any time of the day and during spring and other good seasons they can have up to about 12 chicks with them – always be aware!

* Near the Yingarrie Bluff and Waukenjerrie Hill (537m) on the western side of the road white quartz covers the ground and soon we come over a rise giving a good vista to the north before we get to Barrambie Homestead turnoff and the Ballanhoe Peaks.

* The Rabbit Proof fence was a failure before it was finished as rabbits had made their

London Bridge near Sandstone has been a popular picnic spot for many years.

LEN ZELL

Emus hitting a car at speed have been known to kill passengers.   LEN ZELL

Meekatharra Creek runs right through town.   LEN ZELL

way too far west quickly. Two more fences were later constructed and are now maintained by the local shires. Just southeast of where this fence crosses the road was the town of Barrambie – a short-lived town to support those who developed mines in the areas due to the gold found by the fence builders in 1905 – maybe we should go fencing!

* Further north scalded black stony country resumes with smaller shrubby vegetation and low herbage. There are sand dunes, well away from the road, on either side in this section then the Colga Downs Road goes off to the west. The boundary between Meekatharra and Sandstone is our next sight.

* Barlongi Rock is a granite dome in the midst of grazing country and fun to climb – just because it's there! It also gives a great panoramic view.

More granite outcrops occur as we go north and there are large areas where the granite is level with the ground – imagine how far a big rock continues under the ground!

* Alongside Quinns Lake and Nowthanna Hill to the west are scalded claypans indicating we are in the lowlands here, we find an opportunity to get out and check the floors of the claypans.

* Gradually coming into view is a massive mullock heap west of the road belonging to big open-cut Gabanthina Mine and Mount Yagahong on the eastern side is one of the few sizable peaks in the region and with the nearby Gabanintha Pool was likely to have been a site of importance for all locals.

* Meekatharra (Aboriginal for 'place of little water') is the largest centre in the Murchison and is where you find the old State Battery, Meekatharra Creek, Royal Flying Doctor Service, School of the Air and government agencies. The heritage walk and museum explain and complement the

A composite panorama of Mt Yagahong has important Aboriginal stories associated with it.

LEN ZELL

many local historical and natural features including gorges, mines, wells, lakes and buildings – all overlying a very rich and important Aboriginal history. This was the first town in Australia to be powered by solar energy when a solar/diesel facility was built in 1982 – the biggest of its time. Its huge 2181m-long airport built by the Americans during WWII can be used as an alternative to Perth's airport. The railhead, now closed, was used to take cattle to Perth after they had been driven to here from the Northern Territory.

The old Nannine townsite is now no more than the old railway siding.

A mining town hidden amongst mullock heaps could be a good way to describe the town. As you approach it the size and colours of these waste heaps is astounding. Note the apparent ages and attempts by plants to recolonise some of them.

Meekatharra to Cue

* Nannine Town site, about 40km south of Meeka (as Meekatharra is known to the locals), is on the shores of another generally-dry salt lake, Lake Annean. Nannine is now little more than the remnants of a well-made stonework railway siding and platform. The quality of workmanship and layout all indicate a sizeable operation up until it was closed in 1978. The railway was opened to here from Cue in 1903. The town was the first proclaimed in the Murchison goldfields (1891), a year after the first gold was found about 10km north of here.

The fortunes of the nearby fields faded by the early 1900s and the railway extension to Meeka in 1910 sparked a little life into the town, which then died out, to be buried by tailings from an open-cut mine nearby.

* Saltbush plains in claypans are part of Lake Annean which we cross on a causeway, whilst on the west side of the road the old rail bed appears and disappears in cuttings, grass and earth.

Lake Nallan filled after recent rains.   LEN ZELL

The Masonic Lodge is one of Cue's   LEN ZELL
historic buildings.

* Soon after the Shire boundary between Mount Magnet and Cue we pass to the east of Mummarra Hill about 1km off the road, and it is part of a ridge running parallel to road for a couple of kilometres – and then we rise up to 475m looking back to the ENE over Mount Yagahong and the nearby Gabanthina Mine site.

* On the east side of the road there are now remains of old concrete railway bridges – all part of the old Mullewa – Mount Magnet – Meekatharra rail line.

* Near the Tuckanarra turnoff there are again many old mines and Tuckanarra Hill (492m) due south.

* About 8km further south we see Lake Nallan on the western side of the road and forested lands continuing past the Nallan Station Stay turnoff.

* Milly Soak is off to the West and during Cue's earliest days their water supply was polluted by their wastes drained into the street and well – the soak supplied carted water. The Soak has always been an important recreational site as well.

* Approaching Cue from the north challenges you to work out which hills are man-made and which are natural? The fact that this is a major gold mining site is obvious.

* Cue, now with a population of about 700, down from the peak of 2000 and up from the low of 350, has always been known as the 'Queen of the Murchison', recognising its title from the halcyon days of the 1890s gold rush. The annual QFest brings Queens of a different type to the area these days! The fortunes of gold won from this harsh landscape have contributed to the old buildings still standing proud in the town – the Gentlemen's Club, now housing the Shire offices and historic photo collection, rotunda, government offices, old goal, railway station and Masonic Lodge.

Prior to its settlement as a mining town the Cue location had always been the site of important large-scale meetings between different Aboriginal nations. Cue is proud of the

A composite panorama of the approach to Cue where it is difficult to pick real and man-made hills.

Wajarri, Badimia, Wutha and Tjupan people who still live here and are very much part of the whole community. Stop in the middle of the street and imagine the debates and battles that ensued over the millennia, leading to the one over the tossing of human wastes into the creek that ran down the main street and polluted the water supply well, which is now said to be under the rotunda. This meant that they had to get water from the Milly Soak out of town. Night carts arrived eventually, ending the typhoid problems.

LEN ZELL

Cue has three cemeteries and all show the difficulties faced by those in these remote towns.

The three Cue cemeteries present a record of deaths by typhoid, camel, mine accidents and many other ways. The first was relocated to the foot of Cue Hill and the present-day one is located half-way between Cue and Day Dawn, to service both, and is a well-maintained and poignant place.

LEN ZELL

Day Dawn Mine was operated until recently almost undermining the old Great Fingal Mining Company's superb building.

* Big Bell townsite was abandoned in the mid-1950s and is marked by the remnants of the old hotel (which was an art-deco duplicate copy of the Como Hotel in Perth), concrete house pads and ruins generally.

* Day Dawn mine townsite, only a few kilometres from Big Bell and about 6.5km from Cue, was dependent on the successes of the Great Fingal Mining Co. which closed its mine in 1918, signalling the end of the town. The old mining office, a magnificent stone building, now sits in lonely splendour on the edge of an open-cut mine.

* Walga Rock is 80km out of town and is an extremely important Aboriginal ceremonial

and art site that needs special consideration and understanding prior to visiting. Our suggestion is to only visit it with an Aboriginal guide on a Thoo Thoo Warninha Aboriginal Corporation tour to ensure best information, appropriate behaviour and access to the appropriate areas. It is a granite monolith about 1.5 km long and 5km around on Austin Downs Station. The nearby Wilga Mia ochre mine has been mined by Aboriginal people for over 30,000 years and its products with the Walga Rock site feature in many aspects of Aboriginal law ceremonies and cultural history. It is said to be the oldest continuously-used mine in the world.

Lake Austin surrounds the hill on which Austin township, now gone, was built.   LEN ZELL

The Granites are an eerie place of granite rocks and caves with level swales in between. A very important Aboriginal site.   LEN ZELL

Cue to Mount Magnet

* About 16km south of Cue we see claypans on both sides of the road until we reach Lake Austin and cross its bed for about 10km. We see it again to the east about 15km further on. There are many abandoned mines scattered throughout this trip, with interesting rolling hills and granite outcrops visible.

* Austin townsite was gazetted in 1895, flourished for many years and by the time the railway had closed down in 1978 the town was long gone. Austin is perched on an 'island' overlooking the salt flats of Lake Austin, which are rich in salt-resistant plants and the animals that thrive in these communities. On those rare occasions when the lake gets water in it, billions of small animals emerge from their encysted eggs and all goes crazy until the water dries up and the dry quiet returns.

* We cross the boundary between Mount Magnet and Cue Shires and pass Wanarie Station to the west and soon get to the holding yards for Mid West Goats – suppliers of goat meat to wholesalers.

* The Granites are an area of major Aboriginal significance 6.5km north of Mount Magnet. This is an area where the decomposing granite has created amphitheatre-type flats between the granite breakaways and incredible shapes of caves, overhangs, slopes and secluded nooks all around. The site is very fragile and needs to be treated with significant respect. If you go into the area please don't touch anything, leave no mess, stay on tracks and respect this important site. The Western Australian Museum is developing a management strategy for the site.

Dawn at the Steep Point camping area.

Kingsford Smith Mail Run

Kingsford Smith Mail Run

Sir Charles Kingsford Smith or 'Smithy' as he is affectionately remembered was one of those characters who apparently was a 'bit of a lad'. Stories abound of his exploits and none so dramatically than of his years as a mail run operator with his partner Keith Anderson, from Carnarvon to the Bangemall goldfields near Burringarra (Mount Augustus). Smithy had flown with Australia's first commercial airline in 1924 and wanted the money to buy his own plane. The mail run suited his ingenuity and adventurous spirit – both were needed to be successful. Campbell and Co. had the run from Meekatharra to Bangemall and between the two carrying operations the mail, supplies and occasional passengers eventually got through.

Sometimes it was a dream run and on others they would be camped out beside their bogged vehicle for weeks until the soil dried out enough to move again. We hope your trip mirrors one of Smithy's best ones, but as you do the run spare him, and the many others, a thought and some thanks. We travel from Meekatharra to Carnarvon.

* Meekatharra (Aboriginal for 'place of little water') is the largest centre in the Murchison and is covered in detail in the Miner's Pathway previously.

* We start off west past the Meeka Power Station before we turn off into Peace Gorge about 2km out of town. Sadly here is a prime example of vandalism, with names painted onto or carved into places of cultural, historical or visual significance. To see such magnificent granite boulders covered in so much graffiti prompts hopes the local agencies will rectify matters soon. This gorge was an important Aboriginal site used for ceremonial gatherings and then became a picnic ground for the miners and their families. It was the focus for the celebration of the end of WWI as the one-in-six men who had left returned home several months later.

* After leaving Peace Gorge low herbage covers fairly scalded grass country with poverty bush less than 1m-high, then gradually changing as we move into a ridge with Acacias to 3m with intermittent patches of quartz-covered stony ground then back to poverty bush to Acacia and vice versa. We see many working termite mounds which appear to be heavily eroded by rain and about 75cm in height.

* About 50km from Meeka there is a small hill to the east of the road which is a great little spot for a short walk. It gives you an outlook over the surrounding district with the low hills to the west and poverty bush plains merging into the Acacia plains.

* A windmill with a stone tank reminds us of the old government-serviced-and-supplied water systems for the drovers and travellers who came through here. Smithy and his partner would have also relied on these.

* Little mullock heaps and termite mounds continue to occur spasmodically – all indicating miners and graziers of a different type!

* We cross the Hope River which leads into the Yalgar, which we cross further along, and it leads into the Murchison.

* After the Koonmarra turnoff to SW there are several little creek crossings and a continuation of the Acacia, poverty bush,

LEN ZELL

Wattles and poverty bush are the dominant plants in this harsh landscape.

e outcrops
e many
cular sights at
Gorge.

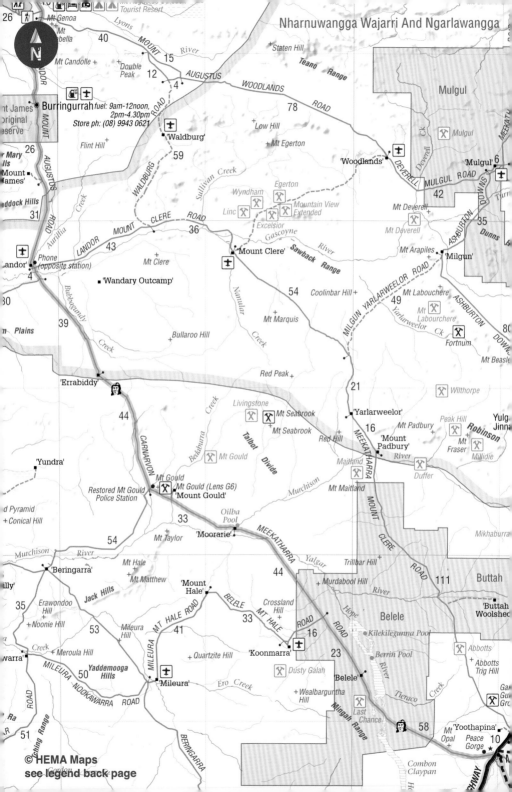

termite mounds and pebble plains graduating into bare plains, then into Acacias with all mixes in between.

* Once you are in amongst River Red Gums and Acacias of a flood plain you know you are in the Yalgar River crossing, which is about 1km across and then we break back into Acacia country.

* Another area of gums and riverine vegetation indicates we are into the channels of the Murchison River, which we drop in and out of several times until we pass Moorarie Homestead to the NE.

* Mount Gould Homestead marks our approach to Mount Gould and you can see how the mine between the two peaks is working its way into both peaks from the saddle between.

The Murchison River channel with the Moorarie Homestead perched above it is a cool respite.

Vegetation changes from the plain onto the Mount Gould slopes are a fabulous example of the effect of exposure and soil and changes. Look at the peaks themselves where the aspect of the slopes causes different vegetation.

* Mount Gould lockup has an amazing history after being established, primarily by the local graziers, in 1888. Plan on spending an hour or so here and go for a wander around and down into the creek – the 'feel' of the place is very strong. The birds coming in for the water and the plants around the tank are interesting to see.

Mount Gould has a mine between it's two peaks.

As the pastoralists moved into this country they were constantly in conflict with the traditional owners and so various 'acceptable' systems of legal process were implemented to resolve the problem. The book *Jandamarra and the Bunuba Resistance* brings a great insight into what this process between the Aboriginal people and graziers meant in the Kimberly. Mention is made of the police from the Mount Gould lockup being moved up to the Kimberley because of their successes

Imagine being dragged into here to spend a few months in chains.

around here, which meant they had run out of work.

Normally Aboriginal 'criminals' who were named by the graziers were brought and held here by the police. Minor offenders served their time here but the serious offenders were faced with some time here and then the 450km trek to the coast. When the police had

Stony ground abuts the small hills.   LEN ZELL

An innovative method of getting the mail over   LEN ZELL
the flooded Gascoyne River at Landor.

enough prisoners they took them to the coast, police on camels, the Aboriginals by foot and in chains for judgement, and often they were sent to Rottnest Island for internment. The definition of a criminal usually meant they were in a group who had killed a sheep for food. Many were simply shot on sight rather than being taken in.

By the early 1900s the lockup had lost its usefulness with the nearby towns taking over. It became a station outcamp before falling into ruin until its restoration in 1987.

* At the shire boundary for Upper Gascoyne and Meekatharra we move back into more gibber plains with a mixture of rough stone and quartz-covered areas and series of rolling hills.

* Watch for several quartz hillocks and neighbouring ground covered by the remnant quartz rocks before we get to Bedarry Creek which runs into the Bubbagundy Creek that runs parallel to the road on the northern side for about 30km before it runs into the Gascoyne River.

* We pass Errabiddy Homestead and after a while get back into the thick, 5-8m mulga and occasional bigger trees.

* Just past the Erong turnoff to the west we reach the riverine vegetation and the Gascoyne River crossing which is about 6km across with the obvious main channel. Here we see a great example of outback ingenuity in the form of an old 44-gallon (200l) drum slung on a cable as a flying fox to get the mail etc across the river in times of flood. It is always hard to imagine these rivers in flood but this reminds us of some of the trials and tribulations they place on those with a schedule. This mail run still operates, leaving Meekatharra every Wednesday. The Aurillia Creek flows into the Gascoyne from the NE at this point and we swing to the NE and run along the western side of the creek.

* On 5km from the main Gascoyne channel we come to the Aurilla Creek crossing which is quite a pleasant stopover point, and then the Landor Homestead on the western side of road and there is a public telephone here. The annual Landor Races are a couple of days of horsing around by hundreds of people and well worth the effort if you can fit it in. They love out-of-towners! Book well ahead.

* The Bore Paddock Hills and Mount Row are due W of the road about 20km north, and about 10km further on is a lovely little rise and granite outcrop on the E side of the road. This is worth a stop and good gaze around to get a perspective of ranges to the west and the general lay of the land.

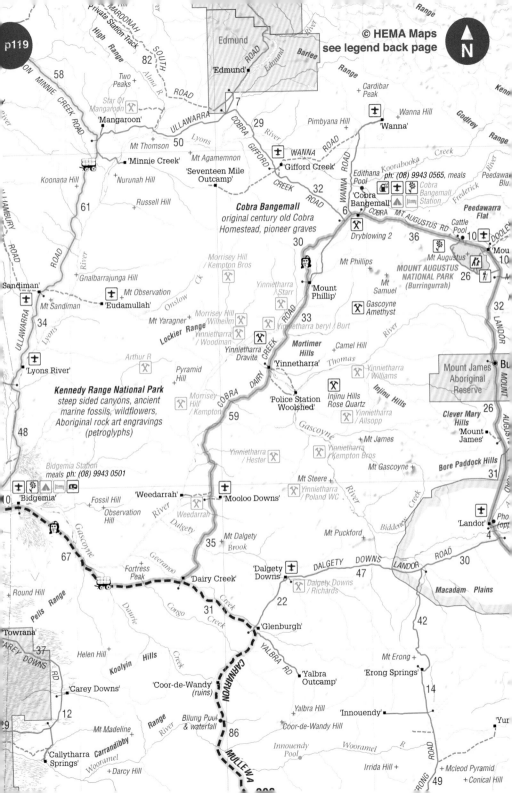

Quartz intrusions into the Burringurrah
sandstones have eroded into square patterns.   LEN ZELL

Vegetation covers most of Burringurrah
reducing its massive size visually.   LEN ZELL

Beedoboondu site was important in Aboriginal
mythology and the rock in the middle of this
creek has important petroglyphs carved
underneath it.   LEN ZELL

* Note the changes around you as you cross the small range known as the Koondoodoo Hills which appear more substantially to the west.

* As we enter the Mount James Aboriginal Land note the interesting little granite breakouts and quartz gibbers over the soil surfaces interspersed with poverty bush, Hakeas and Acacias

* The Burringurrah Aboriginal Community is a settlement of 200-250 people and you need to call ahead to check the shop hours if relying on them for food or fuel.

* After crossing the southern boundary of Cobra Station we cross an interesting range called the Pink Hills and then the Thomas River.

* No matter which way you approach Burringurrah, also known as Mount Augustus, any of the hills we have been seeing are pushed into insignificance compared to the mighty Burringurrah! Note the strata in the rocks in the hills all around us and imagine them projected out over the top of Burringurrah to get idea of how much land was above the rock at some time in the past

Burringurrah is well known as the largest monolith in the world, being two and a half times bigger and three times older than Uluru (Ayer's Rock), stands 1015m high and 8km long and covers about 5,000ha. It consists of 1,650-million-year-old granite with 1 billion-year-old conglomerates on top. The whole mass was pushed up into a fold and the nearby lands eroded away, leaving half of the fold sloping into the sky – called a monocline. Due to its vegetation and slopes of eroded material at its base, Burringurrah lacks the immediate visual impact of Uluru.

Those who take the time to see this magnificent landmark, Burringurrah, in its entirety and in the light of its Wadjari Aboriginal history will go away well satisfied. The Wadjari have three stories recounting the formation of Burringurrah, each having a component explaining the apparent lying-body-with-a-spear sticking out of a thigh and slash marks on the torso which can be seen from the southeast – all probably used at an appropriate time to strengthen an aspect of the teller's messages to the listener – a usual oral history procedure. Should you take the time and make the effort there are several exceptional Aboriginal guides here who can give you an insight into the allowable information associated with the art and features.

There is also a rich European history associated with the National Park which was declared over 9,168ha in 1989. An accommodation and caravanning facility lies just out of the northeast side of the National Park. A

49km drive runs around the base of Burringurrah and provides access to the various access roads, tracks and interpretive facilities and to several important Aboriginal sites.

Vegetation is primarily tall open mulga scrubland interspersed by larger shrubs, including Gidgee, Miniritchie and Sandplain Wattles, and River Red Gums near water. During wet periods Burringurrah takes on a green colouring as the new plants sprout and the old get new leaves. Soon after the rains, usually in winter and spring, wildflowers bloom, bringing the area to life in a blaze of colour.

Goolinee or Cattle Pool, is one of a string of waterholes in the Lyons River here.

Dingoes, Euros, Long-tailed Dunnarts, Echidnas, Spinifex Hopping Mice, Common Rock Rats and Red Kangaroos can be seen by those taking the time to look carefully or lucky enough to be around during the researcher's trapping programs. Snakes, geckos, skinks, dragons and monitors are common. Over 100 bird species are recorded for the park.

* Goolinee is the original name for Cattle Pool in the Lyons River to the north of Burringurrah. It was used constantly by the Aboriginal people and then later by the pastoralists who moved here 20 years after it was 'discovered' by Francis Gregory in 1858 . It was used up until the 1950s as an important stock route stop, watering cattle and sheep on their way to Meekatharra railhead before trucks took over. There are a series of these pools right along this section of the river, with Goolinee the best.

* Emu Hill Lookout allows a great view of Burringurrah either at sundown or sunrise. Note the way in which the rocks here are large and not worn – still fresh from the mountain, it appears. Note also the changes in the soil, vegetation and other features in the landscape around you.

Mighty Burringurrah's moods change with the sun's angle.

* Kingsford Smith and his partner's contract ended their run at the old Bangemall Inn, which was originally called Euranna. There is an old mine in the hills behind the inn. The new owners are developing interpretive facilities and guided tours to complement their fuel supplies, food and accommodation. Here the generosity of the local Wadjarri people was shown when famous author Bert Facey was rescued by them in 1909. The building is listed by the National Trust and holds an historic wayside inn licence. Every fortnight Smithy or

Edithana Pool is one of several in this section   LEN ZELL
of the Lyons River.

Even from many kilometres away Burringurrah   LEN ZELL
dominates the landscape.

his partner would arrive with the mail and it was apparently a good chance for a party to develop!

The Bangemall Inn is on the western bank of the creek after you have traversed through a series of watercourses and ridges with hard black stony soils and occasional quartz and other rock outcrops and some plains, with the quartz stones 5-6cms in diameter.

* Edithana pool about 15kms from the inn is on the Lyons River, 4-5kms long and 50m wide, providing a superb swimming, picnicking and rest spot. Wedge-tailed Eagles, ibis, corellas and other bird species hang about the water. The River Red Gums and other river vegetation add to the cool oasis-in-the-desert effect.

* We travel SW then into sandier soils and the scrubby country now becoming so familiar, and the further we go the more we see flatter alluvial plains. These tend to be stony, rocky, pebbly and sandy flats changing from one to the other and sometimes the vegetation shifts to match the soils and at other times not.

* Keep looking back to the east where it is possible to see the series of small ranges linking into Burringurrah and the fold effect that generated its structure with the same ridges either side of the road, showing the long, linear continuation of the fold.

A lot of people tend to rush through these places far too quickly, but by taking time and staying at the station stays throughout the routes it is possible to get much greater in-depth understanding of the culture of the people and the yarns that abound about the local heroes, be they the Charles Kingsford Smiths, Aboriginal people or the early explorers. One of the best ways to get these yarns is to sit around a camp fire with a warm drink after a satisfying meal.

* Note soil changes into quite a different vegetation style and colour of rocks and soil and then a continuation of white quartz rocks 3-5cm in diameter and occasional quartz and granitic outcrops through a rolling landscape – sparse poverty bush and Hakea to about 3m.

* After the Mount Phillip turnoff to the east, running parallel and continuing for about 3kms is House Creek, you can see the tops of the Red River Gums through the Acacia scrub, which is now 3-4 metres high.

* At Thirty Three River there are more River Red Gums in a typical mid-west creek crossing and an interesting junction with another creek.

* More sandy flat soils with 4m Acacias with poverty bush in between and the occasional quartz outcrop and white quartz-covered rocky ground.

* Near Yinnetharra Homestead we cross the Gascoyne

River which has a green metal tower which is a river gauging station allowing accurate prediction of downstream river heights during flood events.

  * Note the stratified outcrops of rock to the south of Yinnetharra Station and then fairly open plains with reasonable density of poverty bush and occasional Acacias.

  * A few kilometres past Coomberoo Creek crossing on the east side of the road are more good outcrops of granites.

  * As we cross Mombo Creek have a look at its structure as there are said to be good waterholes along it – sadly well away from the road. The interesting series of hills and ranges on both sides of the road with some quartz exposures and what looks like metamorphosed rock, all show how we are approaching the edge of the plateau. Further along is a continuation of picturesque rolling plains and valleys providing interesting relief – with Acacia shrubs with quartz and other stony or pebbled plains

  * From the Mooloo Creek crossing onwards the view of Mount Dalgety is getting better – if you see a good shot, get it now, then we pass the Mooloo Downs Homestead turnoff as the rolling hills continue.

  * The Mount Dalgety lookout offers a closer view of the range. It is at this point that we make the transition from one geological complex to another. We are moving south from the unweathered igneous rocks, harder rocky soil types and stony plains with hills and mountains breaking the flat horizons of the Archaean Province, into the low relief, flatter more open area of softer rocks and clay soils with distinct creeks – the Permian Basin.

  * After crossing Dalgety Brook there are again some good shots of Mount Dalgety.

  * We turn west after Dairy Creek Homestead onto the Carnarvon Road, and back into claypan country. For a comprehensive description of this road to Gascoyne Junction see the Wool Wagon Pathway section.

There is a relativity of beauty in landscapes – in the eyes of the beholder – the more you look the better you will understand and the more beautiful it becomes. Take the time and develop your technique reading this landscape.

  * The 200km run to Carnarvon heads slightly north of west for 200km and remains parallel to the Gascoyne River all the way. Kingsford Smith and other travellers opened up this route – tied to that scarce resource, water. It also makes sense to travel along a relatively flat route near the river and along between dunes, rather than over them.

  * As we pass Jimba Jimba Station a small low range appears to the north and red-sand dunes begin soon after, running parallel in a NW-SE direction. Well developed claypans

LEN ZELL

Mt Dalgety is almost on the boundary between the Yilgarn Plateau and the lower plains.

Claypans are variable according the muds, sands, clays or dryness.   LEN ZELL

Water ripples aid the rapid evaporation of these shallow waters.   LEN ZELL

Rocky Pool has sustained many in times past and still does today.

occur in the flat areas between the dunes. Subtle variations in the dune vegetation occur and it can be seen to be quite different from the interdunal swales.

* Crossing some dunes gives us good overviews in all directions as we change from the dunes to sand plain areas with 5-8m Acacias and poverty bushes intermittent. We see a few creek crossings with small river gums.

* Just before Mooka Homestead we cross the boundary between the Gascoyne and Carnarvon Shires

* Continuation of Acacia and poverty bush and Cotton-tail Mulla Mulla continues and dunes are now appearing further apart due to our direction of travel. Note how the road direction changes to take advantage of the long flat areas between the dunes. Smithy and his mates would have loved these sections, giving them a respite from the tough bits over dunes and through creek crossings.

* We cross an offshoot gas pipeline which runs EW to Carnarvon from the 1530km Dampier to Bunbury natural gas pipeline, feeding from offshore in the Carnarvon Basin.

* Rocky Pool is a beautiful deep section of the Gascoyne River with interesting rocks, sand bars and overhanging gum and paperbark trees. It has become increasingly popular for picnics and undoubtedly was an important stop for the travellers of old and was very important for the traditional owners of this land.

* The old Carnarvon Post Office is now a restaurant, still the end of the Kingsford Smith Mail Run.

LEN ZELL

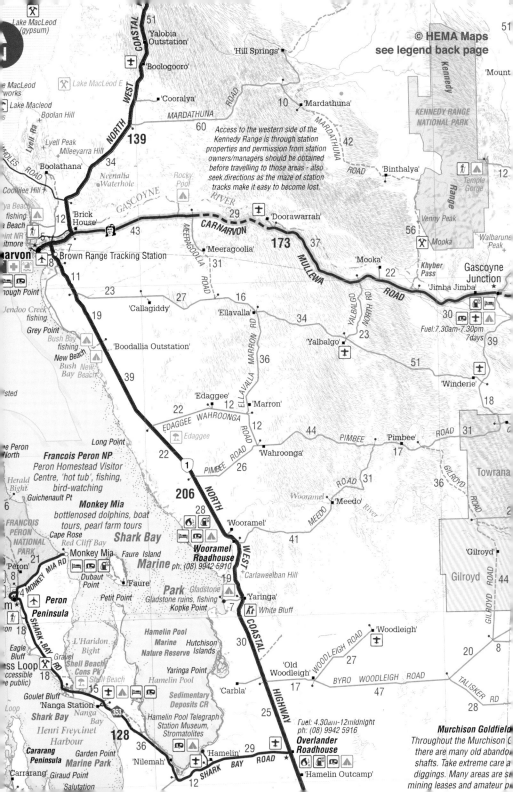

	Geraldton	Mullewa	Yalgoo	Mt Magnet	Paynes Find	Cue
ACCOMMODATION						
Caravan Park	★	★	★	★		★
Bed & Breakfast	★					★
Back Packers	★					
Hotel / Motel Accommodation	★	★	★	★	★	★
Self Contained Units	★		★	★		★
Station Stays		★	★	★	★	★
FACILITIES						
Fuel	★	★	★	★	★	★
Public Restrooms	★	★	★	★	★	★
Auto Repairs	★	★		★		★
Newsagency	★	★		★		★
Postal Service	★	★	★	★		★
Banking	★					
Pharmacy	★					
Public Telephone	★	★	★	★	★	★
Laundromat	★					
Supermarket	★	★		★		★
Nursing Post			★	★		★
Hospital	★	★		★		
Ambulance	★	★	★	★		★
Airport	★	★		★		★
TOURIST INFO						
Tele Centre	★	★	★	★		★
Tourist Centre	★	★	★	★		★
Shire Office	★	★	★	★		★

	Meekatharra	Sandstone	Gascoyne Junction	Murchison Settlement	Carnarvon	Exmouth
ACCOMMODATION						
Caravan Park	★	★	★	★	★	★
Bed & Breakfast		★		★	★	
Back Packers					★	★
Hotel / Motel Accommodation	★	★	★		★	★
Self Contained Units	★				★	★
Station Stays			★	★	★	★
FACILITIES						
Fuel	★	★	★	★	★	★
Public Restrooms	★	★	★	★	★	★
Auto Repairs	★		★		★	★
Newsagency	★				★	★
Postal Service	★	★	★	★	★	★
Banking	★				★	★
Pharmacy					★	★
Public Telephone	★	★	★	★	★	★
Laundromat					★	★
Supermarket	★	★		★ Takeaway Meals	★	
Nursing Post		★	★	★ First Aid Available		
Hospital	★	★			★	★
Ambulance	★	★			★	★
Airport	★	★		★ Airstrip	★	★
TOURIST INFO						
Tele Centre	★	★		★	★	★
Tourist Centre	★	★		★	★	★
Shire Office	★	★	★	★	★	★

Plants

Plants

Some of the features you need to use to identify plants include size, shape, location, bark colours and texture, trunk colours and texture, flowers in detail and the leaf stems and arrangements (the leaves of wattles are petioles which are modified leaf stems). Then note fruit and leaf shapes, numbers on each stem, colour, smoothness, venation, hairiness and texture. With all this together you can then decide categorically which species is which. Alternatively you can be like most of us and use a specific guide book and get a rough idea as to which is which!

Coppercups are one of the spectacular flowers found in the region.

Most travellers are more interested in the weird, cute and cuddly animals in this arid area. Plants get their own back in wildflower season, offering a stunning range of blooms and meadows of colour which capture the attention of all. Colourful everlastings, Parakeelyas, peas, daisies, bush tomatoes and many others create an amazingly, vibrant floral mosaic – often in sharp contrast to the red or white sand and soils. And for the photographer they don't run, swim, slither or fly away when being photographed!

There are over 2200 species of plants in this region. With more than 50 marine algae species, 12 seagrasses, a dozen ferns and the rest flowering land plants, it is an interesting area. This composition of species reflects the rainfall and soils and as there are two overlapping vegetation provinces here – the temperate southern and tropical northern – we get an increase in species seen. Adding to this complexity is the gradation between coastal and desert species as we move eastwards onto the higher lands and different soils.

Flowering shrubs and ground cover are a feast for honeyeaters and insects.

Throughout the whole of the Gascoyne region the native vegetation is simple, dominated by spinifex, wattle (Acacia species – some called mulga) or poverty bush and then varying combinations of all three. Greener vegetation is always a stark contrast to neighbouring forms at springs, soaks, along rivers and their flood plains where eucalypts and paperbarks dominate. The once common clumps of Sandalwood are close to becoming a rarity due to over-harvesting.

Coastal mangrove communities here are scrubby as they are at the limits of their range, generally preferring wetter tropical conditions found to the north. The Grey Mangrove is by far the most common species.

Shrubs and hummocky grass are the dominant species on the sandy dune areas. To the north, the red dune systems often look more like central Australia! As we move into the southern areas the plains have more yellow dunes with Eucalypts, Hakeas and cypress pines

Could we be in Central Australia – no just off Burkett Road!   LEN ZELL

Sturt's Desert Pea is often by the roadside.   LEN ZELL

interspersed with saltbush and samphire communities in the low-lying salt pans, coastal flats and lakes. In Shark Bay are eucalypt woodlands, birrida herb fields, heaths and Acacia shrublands. Along the coast we get samphire flats leading into algal mats and mangrove communities that again lead into the marine algae and seagrass communities.

The Red and Green Kangaroo Paws are two of about 230 species living at the northern limit of their range, while 56 species (including the Rock Fig) are living at their southern limit. This area provides Western Australia's most clearly-defined overlap in flora in a small area.

Almost 100 of the plant species are weeds and some of these are having severe local impacts, especially along rivers. Cape Range has only about 30 weeds and in areas of Shark Bay World Heritage area, understorey weeds have succeeded due to the grazing impacts – of sheep and rabbits removing native species. There are more than a dozen plant species which are considered endangered and many endemic species within the region.   As you travel north you will continue to see many of the dominant species seen at Shark Bay, and this link continues to Cape Range as they have over 300 species in common. Although Cape Range has fewer recorded species (approximately 650) than Shark Bay, it is an incredible number considering this is an arid limestone environment.

Cape Range comes within the Carnarvon Botanical District and its flora is dominated by desert species. Studies have shown floral composition comparisons give close links with Barrow Island and the Burrup Peninsula to the north and Lake MacLeod to the south. At Cape Range there are 50 species living at their northern limit. These northern limited plants are generally found on the sand plains or the coastal dunes on the western side, but not generally on the limestone hills.

The area around Yardie Creek also provides an interesting floristic insight into the past with what are known as disjunct or relict species – ones that are found away from their common distribution area. These include several emergent freshwater species and the Millstream Palm.

Grazing and land clearing has removed many species known by the Aboriginal people as bush tucker. All parts of plants were important for food, medicines and ceremonial purposes. The encyclopaedic botanical knowledge of the Aboriginal people allowed them to make maximum use of scarce resources available in this arid environment. In addition, their knowledge of when to collect and how to prepare the plant products allowed them to eat species that are toxic or partially-toxic if eaten without processing. Recent research has developed knowledge of the higher vitamin, protein and fat levels in native foods, explaining why the Aboriginal people fared so well on what appeared to be a meagre diet.

Aboriginal people also practised a form of agriculture, where they would carefully harvest, then often replant when collecting – thus ensuring a continuous supply of their bush tucker plants. This knowledge was passed on and supported by stories that ensured the sustainability of the species.

MANGROVES

There are six species found on the Shark Bay-Ningaloo Coast with the most common shown here. Due to the severity of the environment and lack of wide uniform environments the typical zonation seen in mangroves elsewhere is less obvious here except on the eastern and southern sides of Exmouth Gulf.

Grey, White or Silver Mangrove – glossy green leaves that are hairy, silver-to-grey under, smooth bark and fragrant orange flowers from November to February with fruits from mid-summer to May. Pencil-like breathing roots erupt vertically from the mud in lines above the horizontal roots.

Red, Stilt or Spider Mangrove – to 10m, very distinctive, creates almost impenetrable tangles, has stilt and aerial roots for support but more so air supply through pores, flowers/fruits February-August, fruit breaks off as seedling to float away. Dark green fleshy leaves make it distinguishable from the grey mangrove.

mangroves provide e habitats.

MARINE PLANTS

LEN ZELL

Mexican Caulerpa – green alga found on sandy or solid substrates, can deflate if any part broken.

SUSIE BEDFORD

Sailor's Eyeball - to 3cr round translucent ball, oft found washed up on beach and mistaken as an anim egg-case, world's large single cell with several sm cells at base.

SUSIE BEDFORD

Turtle Weed - bright-green filamentous algae, grows in tufts, often has bright-green commensal crab within, turtles not known to eat it!

Funnel Weed - distinctive i rolled margins on leav where new growth occu common in seagrass areas a on reefs, washed up beaches.

SUSIE BEDFORD

Brown, red and green algae - easily seen in the intertidal zone, all algae attach with holdfasts as they have no roots, often washed ashore after storms.

SUSIE BEDFORD

Sea Grapes - leafy, cypress feather are forms, green al prostrate creeping shoo root-like rhizoids attach substrate, erect branches, broken whole colony deflat

SUSIE BEDFORD

Sargassum - small floats led to the Portuguese name Sargassum meaning grapes; attaches to substrate, but large pieces often wash up on beaches dragging coral rocks with them.

SUSIE BEDFORD

Disc Algae - algae wi "limestone" skeleton, wh dead leave white skelet major contributor to sands some areas, especially reefs.

SUSIE BEDFORD

Green Sponge Weed – lobed solid masses formed by turgid filaments jamming together, commonly seen on beaches.

LEN ZELL

Seagrasses - flowering pla that live in the sea - have roc stems and leaves - importa food source for many anim including Dugong and turt - important habitat for oth organisms - stabilize t muddy/sandy substrates.

EACH PLANTS

N ZELL

Beach Spinifex - clumps and masses to 1m, commonly first coloniser of beach sands, female flowers rolling along as spiky ball, underground runners help spread plants.

LEN ZELL

Beach Morning Glory or Goat's-foot Convolvulus - showy pink/purple flowers on trailing vine, a colonising plant that helps to stabilise dune and trap sand for other plants.

SIE BEDFORD

Saltbush - densely-leaved shrub with grey hairy leaves, dense flower spikes produce a pungent, almost sickly sweet odour, tends to colonise the primary dunes.

SUSIE BEDFORD

Woolly-button Dune Plant - small silver hairy leaves and dense yellow 'button' flowers.

ALT FLAT SPECIES

N ZELL

Samphire - several species of low shrubs, succulent, to 1m, woody base in old ones, miniscule flowers in joints, edible raw or cooked but very salty, on salt flats.

LEN ZELL

White Pigface - prostrate spreader with succulent green leaves and showy daisy like flowers, Aboriginal people eat the fleshy fruits, seeds spread by Emus and some mammals

LAND PLANTS

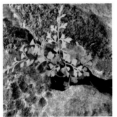

SUSIE BEDFORD

Ferns – 12 species in region - as ferns tend to like moist environments this area does not have abundant fern species, found near waterholes and creeks.

LEN ZELL

Spinifex – provide coole higher-humidity micr environments inside th clumps with many anima relying on these. Smell resin distinct, when burnt, black resin residue is left an used for glues.

LEN ZELL

Ring or Wreath Leschenaultia - prostrate plant to 1m across, dense mass of yellow-deep pink tubular flowers, grow on outside of plant forming a ring which looks like a wreath.

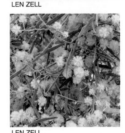

LEN ZELL

Wattles - Mulgas (Acacias) characteristic fluffy-yello flowers in globular heads 'tails', leaves variable from sm oval-shaped to needle-lik seeds need fire to germinat Aboriginal people collect an use seeds used to make flour.

LEN ZELL

River Red Gum - large eucalyptus (gum) tree to 25m, found growing around pools and along seasonal watercourses, Australia's most widespread eucalypt, white flowers September-October.

SUSIE BEDFORD

Green Bird Flower - Parr Plant - Sandhill Rattlepod member of the pea famil shrub with velvety stem distinctive long-keeled, gree flowers with thin black line long hairy ovate leaves, whe shaken dry pods create rattlir sound.

SUSIE BEDFORD

Tamarisk tree - large trees, she-oaks, not native to area but used widely on North West Cape as shade trees, cut branches used as brush to stabilise dunes

SUSIE BEDFORD

Mistletoe - semi-parasit shrub living off sap of ho trees, usually on eucalypt seeds spread by Mistlet Bird, showy red-oran flowers in summer.

LEN ZELL

Flannel bush or bush tomato - characteristic purple flowers with yellow centres, leaves usually furry and stems often thorny -fruit 'bush tucker' for Aboriginal people, several species.

SUSIE BEDFORD

Eucalypts - Australian icons tall trees with long, ov pointed leaves, produce 'gu nuts' containing the seed leaves of some species used make eucalyptus oil, ma species.

Orange Banksia - dense shrub with bright-orange cylindrical flower spike, leaves with large bi-lateral serrations or teeth.

ISIE BEDFORD

LEN ZELL

Sandhill Spider Flower - a shrub to tree (3-6m) grevillea with creamy/pale yellow spider flowers in cylindrical clusters, grows on red sand dunes.

Orange Spider Flower (Grevillea) - clusters of flowers bright-yellow to orange, thin, almost cylindrical, sharply-pointed leaves, shrub 2-6m growing on sand dunes.

N ZELL

SUSIE BEDFORD

Camel Bush or Northern Bluebell - straggly erect herb to 1m - pointed oblong hairy leaves and pale blue lobed flowers in clusters.

Senna (formerly Cassias) - rounded shrub to 1m, silvery leaves, bright-yellow flowers, long green pods, throughout Australia, Aboriginal people eat grubs in roots, use flowers for rituals, burn leaves for insect repellent smoke.

ISIE BEDFORD

LEN ZELL

Paperbarks - found beside many fresh water holes and creeks, soft bark used by Aboriginal people for many purposes, fragrant flowers.

Coastal Caper - shrub to 3m, early morning and evening white flowers with very visible white, erect showy stamens, during day, flowers not so visible as petals and stamens droop, turning pink/purple.

ISIE BEDFORD

SUSIE BEDFORD

Pink Native Hibiscus - tall shrub with pale mauve/pink hibiscus type flower with dark-red centre, leaves 3-lobed or ovate.

Sturt's Desert Pea - pink variety found on North West Cape, same as red form, flowers a beautiful pink.

ISIE BEDFORD

LEN ZELL

Sturt's Desert Pea - small prostrate shrub with pinnate leaves, bright-red pea flowers often with very dark-red to black centres, first collected by William Dampier in 1699.

LAND PLANTS

LEN ZELL

Common Rock Fig - small tree to 6m, smooth pale bark, aerial and clinging roots, red-purple edible fruit to 1.5cm across, roots cling to rocks and grow into cracks.

LEN ZELL

North West Cape Kurrajong - endemic to North West Cape - small deciduous tree with tangle of branches, lobed leaves, small cream flower conspicuous pods when dry without its leaves looks a little like a thin Boab Tree.

LEN ZELL

Parakeelya - prostrate herb with purple/pink flowers with 5 petals and bright-yellow, pollen bearing anthers, very showy during 'wildflower season'.

LEN ZELL

Purple or Tall Mulla Mulla herb with purple flower heads, cone-shaped becoming cylindrical, thick oval leaves ending in point one of more than 35 species.

SUSIE BEDFORD

Poison Morning Glory - small prostrate trailing vine with characteristic 'morning glory' flower, toxic to stock, tuber roots eaten by Aboriginals, often seen on road verges.

LEN ZELL

Brachycome Daisy - erect herb with masses of bluey purple daisy flowers, long thin leaves.

SUSIE BEDFORD

Dune Wattles - characteristic yellow fluffy globular flower, dark green oval leaves on shrub to 2.5m, bushy to ground, common in over-grazed areas.

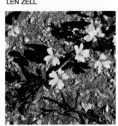
LEN ZELL

Prostrate Goodenia prostrate trailing herb flowers with 5 yellow & white lobed petals along stem leaves hairy and toothed.

LEN ZELL

Sandalwood – to 4m, semi-parasitic plant, aromatic smoke when burnt, sold to Asian markets. See page 88

LEN ZELL

Spotted Fuchsia – Boobialla family, to 3m, with many species, includes poverty, tar turkey, Emu & varnish bushes.

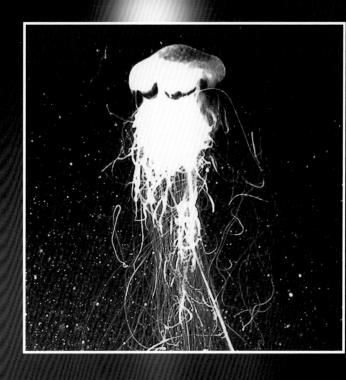

Animals

Animals

At least a dozen scorpion, 350 spider, 20 centipede, 15 millipede, 15 frog, 20 gecko, 16 dragon, 60 skink, four goanna, 16 snake, 300 bird (about two thirds breeding), 15 bat, and 40 non-flying mammal (10 are introduced) species have been found in this massive area so far. Smaller mammals have been almost totally removed from the mainland, which makes the Eden and Heirisson Prong Projects and the refuge islands that the source animals for breeding populations are drawn from, all the more important.

Goats, foxes, cats and rabbits are the most commonly-seen feral animals – all having dramatic impacts in their own ways. Dingoes are also recent arrivals, having been brought into Australia five to eight thousand years ago.

Native and therefore feral animal populations are totally dependent on the habitats that provide their homes, food and water. As all the habitats of the mainland have been dramatically altered by the fire and grazing activities of humans, it is almost impossible to gain a clear picture of what the habitats were like before human occupation and certainly since European arrival. When contemplating this issue, do we consider the pre-Aboriginal landscape more than 50,000 years ago or just the pre-European landscape of, in this area, pre-1850s? Some species, like the Red Kangaroo, have benefited from European settlement due to access to extra water and some pasture improvements. Smaller mammal species however, have been made extinct or had their ranges dramatically reduced on the mainland and most islands.

You are almost guaranteed to see Red Kangaroos and Euros daily – either dead on the roadside, resting in the shade or moving at dawn or dusk. Emus, corellas, Wedge-tailed Eagles and Galahs are also regularly seen. If you see the processional caterpillars check them out close-up and see if you can find their silk trail after they have gone. Ants and spiders will also be seen by observant people.

Habitat diversity means animal diversity so in this region we have desert species inland, burrowing frogs all over, mangrove mudskippers and sea snakes on the coastal areas and then Dugong, Whale Sharks, whales, dolphins, turtles and fish on the coast and out to sea.

The enormous number of species belonging to these groups haven't even been found, let alone studied and named from this region. There are at least 181 species in 62 genera of corals, over 170 species of

Monitors are easy to see out here – they have no trees to climb!

ELL

Watching wildlife

There is a lot out there – but only if you look and use the right gear. When inspecting anything, from minute crustaceans in the algae on the reefs or rocks to Humpback Whales you can use a pair of binoculars to get the best results! Reverse them to use as a strong hand lens. Planning for your experience is important and then the rest is up to that unreliable and exciting element – the wildlife.

LEN ZELL

Your planning needs to include the guides to different groups of animals, Tide Tables, local knowledge of water depths, currents and locations, regional guide-books and brochures. Try to develop some knowledge of the animals and their behaviour and maybe how-and-when to watch them before you go. Essential is good equipment including binoculars, hand lenses, hides, techniques and excellent patience, plus a capacity to instantly react to a call such as – 'Dugong surfacing on port bow!' Always keep in mind that after hearing that call there is a good chance you will still not see it!

Researchers have found the Shark Bay area to be one enormous and pleasurable laboratory. Not only are there unusual assemblages of organisms but also an environment which aids their study. Substantial research into Dugong, Tiger Sharks, turtles, seagrasses, many fish species and overall ecosystem studies have been successfully undertaken and continue. The Project Eden and Heirisson Prong Projects are world leaders and essential for our understanding of ecosystem recovery processes, so all in all this continues as a great study area.

Due to the overlap of the southern and northern bio-regions here, the whole intermixing of their faunas makes for an interesting experience.

While travelling as you are looking for one animal or plant feature, try to have others searching for different things as your search pattern will block out all others – so have eg, one person on flowers, one for birds, one for other animals and one for rocks.

echinoderms, more than 540 species of molluscs, over 200 species of decapods and 50 species of barnacles in the crustacea, up to 800 species of polychaete worms are expected – and so on it goes. Mostly small, these animals are ignored by many and as a consequence some of the most bizarre and wonderful aspects of our animal kingdom are missed. Learn to crawl around with a good hand lens and enjoy!

In the arid lands insects are abundant and all have amazing strategies to survive the extremes of heat, dry periods and cold. Some hibernate as pupae and others encyst to survive the long dry periods. Almost all have fast life cycles to allow them to grow and breed in a short time while there is water about. Spiders are common and yet rarely seen by many. This is another poorly-known group with the orb weavers, huntsmen and tarantulas the most commonly seen. Great websites are www.calm.gov.au/plants_animals and www.museum.wa.gov.au/faunabase

MARINE INVERTEBRATES

Black sponge - primitive aggregations of single cells, diverse shapes, colours and can exude toxins. Also branching and encrusting forms.

EN ZELL

Ball or basket sponges pump enormous volumes of water filtering out food. Have many commensal animals living on surface.

LEN ZELL

Hair jelly or snotty - jellies have many shapes, sizes, colours and tentacle toxic levels to capture prey.

EN ZELL

Staghorn coral clump form, note terminal polyp on each branch, other individuals down sides, thousands of animals in this colony.

LEN ZELL

Anemones share animal shape with corals and hydroids, occur only as single individual, often with commensal clown fish. Can sting.

USIE BEDFORD

Golf ball and honeycomb corals have bigger polyps, the animals, retracted here and farming the single-celled plants called zooxanthellae living in their tissue.

LEN ZELL

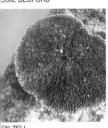

Plate staghorn coral - fast-growing group contributing much to reef growth.

EN ZELL

Kidney or boulder coral - can form colonies five metres across and thousands of years old. Grow at up to 2cm per year.

LEN ZELL

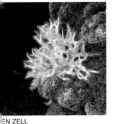

Tubeworm - unusual one that lives as a colony making a fragile, branching skeleton.

EN ZELL

Christmas-tree Worm - exposes gills for feeding and breathing, retract very quickly if disturbed.

LEN ZELL

MARINE INVERTEBRATES

LEN ZELL

Goose or stalked barnacles - attach to floating logs, ropes and pumice in open ocean waters, carried long distances.

SUSIE BEDFORD

Tidepool barnacles - four on rocks, piles, turtles and whales, are basically a crab on their back. Shore or rock crabs usually run and hide before you get to them.

SUSIE BEDFORD

Crinoids or feather stars are filter feeders spreading their food capturing arms into the currents.

SUSIE BEDFORD

Ghost crab - most common beach burrow digger. Feed on anything dead on the beaches.

LEN ZELL

Hermit crab - shells on any beach are very important to allow these crabs to have a home. Many found inland in dunes a hundred metres from the sea.

SUSIE BEDFORD

Red-eyed Crab - reef top dweller - very aggressive feeds on detritus.

SUSIE BEDFORD

Sea hare - up to 30cm long and cruise around reef tops and sand, exude purple dye if annoyed.

LEN ZELL

Baler Shells - can reach 75cm animal length - here cruising over sand looking for prey below.

LEN ZELL

Limpets amongst rockpool barnacles. The limpets are molluscs that graze the algae on the rock surfaces and return to same place.

LEN ZELL

Periwinkles occur in the spray and splash zones of many rocky shores.

MARINE INVERTEBRATES

N ZELL

Black nerites - cluster together on many rocky shores to keep moisture on hot days.

SUSIE BEDFORD

Money Cowries occur on most coral reefs and were used as currency in some cultures. The soft mantle keeps the shell clean and growing.

N ZELL

Rock oysters have two shells, bivalves, filter feeders and popular to eat.

LEN ZELL

Black mussels can be found on the sandy flats in Shark Bay.

N ZELL

Giant Clams - found on most tropical reefs, have been overharvested in many countries. Symbiotic algae in animal tissue produces excess calcium carbonate dumped into shell.

SUSIE BEDFORD

Sea stars have many shapes and colours, feed on coral, detritus and algae. Many species.

N ZELL

Sea urchins have beautifully articulated spines on ball and socket joints, move around with sucker-like tube feet.

SUSIE BEDFORD

Sea cucumbers are know as the 'vacuum cleaners' of the sea, pick up sand, eat it and digest food from amongst grains.

N ZELL

Sea squirts occur as individuals and many as encrusting colonial forms. Larvae have a primitive backbone.

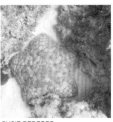

SUSIE BEDFORD

Pin Cushion Stars - also a sea star but with very fat arms, feed on corals, algae and detritus.

TERRESTRAIL INVERTEBRATES

LEN ZELL

Moths find mates by scent, eggs laid on host plant and hatch into herbivorous caterpillars that pupate into adult.

LEN ZELL

Butterflies are colourful da flying moths which fir mates by sight. Pupae ha from vegetation. Adults fe on nectar, sap or don't feed all.

LEN ZELL

Mosquitos are common and are small flies with long proboscis to feed on blood, aquatic larvae.

Grasshoppers dig into t soil to lay 10-200 eggs, hat into little hoppers then aft four moults adults will fly.

LEN ZELL

LEN ZELL

Land Snails
Land snails occur in many areas and their shells under the Spinifex on the Ningaloo Coast indicate large numbers at times. Come out to feed and breed after rain.

LEN ZELL

Dragonflies, 195 species Australia, many colours ar sizes, eat many mosquitos adults and larvae.

Termites are insects with sophisticated earthen mounds with temperature and humidity controls, eat grass and leaves. Single pair starts colony.

LEN ZELL

LEN ZELL

Praying mantis - voracio predators eating small insects.

Crickets are closely related to grasshoppers, also lay eggs in the soil, have wingless nymphs and rasp wings and legs making sounds.

LEN ZELL

LEN ZELL

Scale insects have lerps waxy secretions that cov them as they suck juices fro the leaves. They are oft attended by ants who e secretions.

RRESTRIAL INVERTEBRATES

ZELL

Orb-weaving spiders are spectacular females seen hanging in webs between trees, often in clusters. Look for very small males nearby.

LEN ZELL

Many burrowing and trap-door spiders can be seen by those who seek them in the sandy soils, use silk to strengthen burrow, ambush their prey at night.

ZELL

Redback Spider –female, can give fatal bite in rare cases, messy small funnel like web, like dry shaded places, males small and usually eaten during mating.

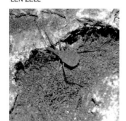

LEN ZELL

Cave fauna have adapted to the lack of light and soil colours. We are yet to get an identification on this one!

ZELL

True bugs have many colours and shapes in their 600 species. Eat sap from leaves and seeds.

LEN ZELL

A weevil beetle found wandering a dune, have chewing mouthparts for seeds.

ZELL

Processional caterpillars can form lines up to 8m and follow a silk trail to a food tree.

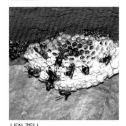

LEN ZELL

Paper nest wasps don't need water to produce the paper for the chambers in which they put paralysed spiders for their larvae to feed upon.

ZELL

Many of the 4000 Australian ant species occur in the region, these foraging meat ants are carrying a dead comrade back to the colonial nest as food.

LEN ZELL

The 'golden-bum' ants belong to the largest genus of ants, live in ground nests, are docile.

Dangerous marine animals

Should any of these animals injure you make immediate contact with your nearest medical professional and follow their instructions. All commercial tour operators are normally required to carry First Aid kits and are trained in their use. If you are exploring this coast privately ensure you have the appropriate First Aid kit, procedures and treatment capacities.

Dangerous Animals - First Aid Hints

There is no substitute for having a good First Aid book and training.

Snake and spider bites
Use pressure-immobilisation as it slows movement of venom from bite into circulation. Place firm pressure over the bitten area and immobilise the limb with firm bandaging.

Box Jelly stings
Pour domestic vinegar (never methylated spirit or alcohol) liberally over the adhering tentacles as soon as possible to inactivate the stinging cells - it does not reduce pain or reverse completed stings. Maintain EAR and CPR as required.

Irukandji *(Carukia barnesi)*
No definitive treatment is currently available. First Aid of analgesia, reassurance and EAR and/or CPR if necessary.

Blue bottle or Portuguese Man-of-war *(Physalia sp.)*
First Aid consists of removal of the tentacles, preferably with forceps. Vinegar is not recommended. Use ice packs and/or topical anaesthetic agents.

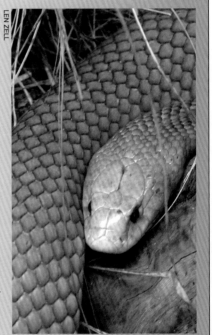

LEN ZELL

Mulga or King Brown is dangerously venomous.

Other types of sea jellies
Vinegar is suitable for most other types of stings. Local pain is usually best treated with ice packs. Analgesia may be required.

Stonefish and stingrays
First Aid consisting of bathing or immersing the stung area in almost boiling-hot water to denature the venom. Do not attempt to restrict the movement of the injected toxin. Take the victim to hospital for immediate treatment, wound cleaning and update of tetanus injection.

Blue-ringed Octopus bites
First Aid is prolonged EAR until the venom wears off.

Cone shell stings
Place a cold pack on the stung area and maintain EAR and CPR until hospitalised.

DANGEROUS MARINE ANIMALS

Fire Coral – 'fire weeds' or stinging hydroids – found in reef areas – three forms have similar stinging cells found in corals, anemones and sea jellies, stings quite painful but only causes minor irritation.

N ZELL

LEN ZELL

Blue Bottles or Portuguese Man-of-War – found floating in coastal waters and their dangling tentacles cause stings.

N ZELL

Anemones – many species, that can all give mild-to-severe stings, often have commensal shrimps or fish. Avoid touching them.

LEN ZELL

Bristle Worms – these are free-living polychaete (many-haired) worms that if handled break off minute hairs in the skin, causing irritation. Sticky tape, wax peel, glue or similar can remove some hairs. Use an anaesthetic to ease pain.

N ZELL

Cone Shells – can inject a fatal toxin by means of a dart used to catch small fish. They are normally found only on coral reefs or fringing reef areas. It is possible for them to fire the dart into you wherever you hold the shell. They can be fatal to humans.

www.BarrierReefAustralia.com

Blue-ringed Octopus – highly-venomous animal grows to 20cm tip-to-tip, lives in small shells, bottles, cans and any space. When disturbed, body is covered in pulsating, iridescent blue rings.

N ZELL

Sea Urchins – are found in nooks and crevices on the rocky shores and reef tops and edges. Always wear strong shoes and be careful where you place your feet. Remove spines and soak in hot water.

LEN ZELL

Stingrays – many species, as you walk in shallows shuffle feet, if trodden on they bend over your foot and drive barb into foot injecting venom. Keep foot in almost-boiling water until the venom is denatured.

N ZELL

Box Jelly - have buds of tentacles on each corner of their bell, range from 1cm to 25cm across, all can kill humans.

LEN ZELL

Moray eels – 15 species in this area, breathing action looks aggressive but only attack if provoked, recurved teeth hold prey efficiently. A fish with long, slender, snake-like body.

DANGEROUS MARINE ANIMALS

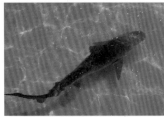

www.monkeymiawildsights.com.au

Sharks – these much-maligned opportunistic feeders are common throughout the region. They have little interest in humans unless you have done something to attract them and even then you are only likely to be hurt as they go for the attraction and you get hit on the way or as they mouth everything to try to find the attraction source. All tropical species are present. Most are harmless and Great Whites are seen as far north as Exmouth.

LEN ZELL

Stone Fish – these are slow-moving, well-camouflaged fish that lie on the bottom looking just like an algae-covered rock. Should you stand on one their dorsal fins they have a venom gland at the base that can inject, giving severe pain. As with stingray venom, keep the area in almost-boiling water for about 25 minutes. This denatures the venom and the pain is reduced.

LEN ZELL

Sea Snakes – these are common and are found in mangrove creeks in the trees, on the mud, in the waters and right out to the coral reefs well off shore. Like terrestrial snakes they are scaly, breathe air and some lay their eggs on shore whilst the fully-marine species give birth to live young that have hatched within the mother. They are slow-moving and placid animals unless you disturb them at mating time or hurt them in some way. They are close relatives of the cobras and strongly venomous. If you are bitten you can die within about 20 minutes, but usually they only bite in self-defence and only envenomate once in about ten bites.

Animals with backbones - Vertebrates

The most memorable of these belong to the charismatic big animals or mega-fauna that get people excited when seen. Most will see the kangaroos, birds, dolphins, turtles, Dugong, monitors, dragons, fish, occasional shark, birds and if lucky the Whale Sharks, bats, flying foxes, and whales that frequent this area. We now know these as wildlife as they usually run upon seeing a human. Could this have something to do with the 80% reduction in large animal species coinciding with a major climate change and the arrival of humans on this continent?

Fishes

There are different species according to where you go – offshore in oceanic waters there are the pelagic species including trevally, tuna, mackerel and billfish and as you come closer to shore the demersal species are found including perch, trout and emperors and further inshore the bottom dwellers such as flathead and whiting are found. It is not unusual to find some species where 'they shouldn't be' as well, which can often indicate a change in currents, a small outcrop of substrate not normally found or just a fish which is lost!

Manta rays tend to cruise around the whole area wherever there is zooplankton and the area is famous for the Whale Sharks that congregate to feed from March to June on the rich coral spawn and zooplankton. Sharks are throughout and include the Oceanic White-tip, Grey Reef, Tiger and Sand Sharks. Numerous other species in all groups occur throughout the region due to the rich diversity of habitats.

The muddy rivers and pools when drier are rich in fish life if only for a small time. Some

HARKS, RAYS AND FISHES

EN ZELL

Sting Rays – feed on shells and crabs in the sand and if trodden on will flick tail over driving a superb barb through the foot – venom denatured by very hot water for 20 minutes.

LEN ZELL

Manta rays feed on the same food as Whale Sharks, are up to 5m across and also harmless.

EN ZELL

Epaulette and Bamboo Sharks – common reef-top dwellers, hide head under coral, teeth rasp-like grating or crushing, males have two claspers beside cloaca.

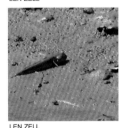

LEN ZELL

Mudskippers can be seen in the mangroves, live in burrows, roll eyes into head to keep them wet, gill pouches keep gills wet to breathe air.

EN ZELL

Whale Sharks are the world's biggest fish, harmless, feeding on microscopic animals called plankton floating in water. Their annual appearance is the focus of a growing tourist industry.

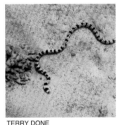

TERRY DONE

Harlequin Snake Eels are often seen, fish so not related to sea snakes, eats small fish and crabs, lives in crevices in coral.

EN ZELL

Cow-tail Rays can be up to 3m long and like smaller cousins have barbed tail with toxic venom which can reach forward to stab.

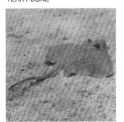

LEN ZELL

Spotted stingrays are commonly seen on sandy lagoon floors all along coast. Venomous barb in middle of tail.

SHARKS, RAYS AND FISHES

SUSIE BEDFORD

Teira Batfish - these juveniles change shape as they mature, graze on algae.

LEN ZELL

Six-banded Angelfish a beautifully adorned at a stages of their changin colours with age, grow t 50cm, eat small animals.

PHIL DODD

Blue-barred Orange Parrot-fish are some of many grazing fish that keep algae-covered surfaces on reefs clean, move over reef top with rising tides.

LEN ZELL

Golden Trevally are swee eating, feed on live pre move to deeper water as the get older and lose vertica bars.

SUSIE BEDFORD

Burrowing Gobies are commonly seen in the lagoon floor sands, you have to wait as they are timid.

SUSIE BEDFORD

Striped Puffer-fish are timi strong-jawed carnivore poisonous flesh, can inflate annoyed.

LEN ZELL

Narrow-barred Spanish Mackerel are one of the most popular game fish on the coast, up to 55kgs, excellent eating, generally seasonal.

LEN ZELL

Brown Demoiselle – slende reef dweller, blue edges o fins, defends territory, alg feeder.

SUSIE BEDFORD

Blackspot Goat Fish – feeds on small animals sensed in sand by chin barbells, usually in small groups.

LEN ZELL

Neon Damsel – plankto feeder, lives among cora distinctive blue colour, pa of "wall of mouths" on edg of reefs.

species occur all year round and others seem to come and go with the rains. Then there are the blind fish found in the waters under Cape Range and its nearby plain.

Reptiles and amphibians

Frogs, the amphibians of the region, are common but rarely seen and emerge like magic after rain. They wait in almost suspended animation until they can burrow to the surface from their protective sac or climb out from the moist spot they survive the dry in. It is then a frantic race against time to find a mate, breed and grow before the water dries up.

There are over 840 described species of reptile in Australia. Snakes, geckos, turtles and lizards are the most common terrestrial reptiles; this is a rich area as their protective skins allow them to thrive in this environment. This region has the highest density of lizards of any arid land in the world. It is common to see the monitors on or near the roads, dragons dashing into hiding from their rock perches, snakes cruising across the road or shinglebacks dawdling into danger on the roads. All prefer cooler times of the day and yet need the warmth of the sun to allow them to hunt effectively with some species feeding only at night. Spinifex clumps host most reptiles with cracks and crevices in the soil, trees and rocks next most important.

Marine Reptiles

These include the sea snakes with the Olive most common and turtles with Hawksbill, Green, Flatback and Loggerheads found here. The Green Turtle is the most common and nesting behaviour and locations are monitored by the Turtle Monitoring Project based in Exmouth. The Turtle Interpretive Centre at Jurabi, and nearby turtle nesting beaches, in Cape Range National Park are well worth a visit along the Jurabi Coast.

e Green
comes
to nest.

AMPHIBIANS AND REPTILES

LEN ZELL

Green Turtles are one of the three species which nest on this coast, lay up to 150 eggs per clutch, graze on sea grasses and algae.

LEN ZELL

Desert Tree Frogs appe with rain or sprinklers, trees, in bathrooms, or ne creeks, breed after summ rains, insectivores.

SUSIE BEDFORD

16 species of spiny-tailed geckos in Australia have distinct spines, repellent liquid squirted from under tail if distressed.

LEN ZELL

Shingleback, **Pinecor Stumpy-tail Lizard** - has scales, mate for life meet ea spring, eat small animals.

LEN ZELL

Central Military Dragons are commonly seen scuttling into safety. Approach carefully and they will sometimes sit still.

LEN ZELL

Ta-ta Lizards lift their fe regularly to keep them cool advertise their territories. E small animals.

SUSIE BEDFORD

Thorny Devils walk with jerky movements, always curved tail, eat ants.

LEN ZELL

Lace Monitor one of species in Australia, forage any foods, swagger arour Lace Monitor lay up to eggs in termite mounds incubate them.

LEN ZELL

Black-headed Pythons occur in wet areas, placid, carnivorous, eating small mammals and frogs.

LEN ZELL

Mulga or King Brown feeds on small mamma reptiles, birds & frogs, lays to 20 eggs, dangerous venomous.

Birds

Some 800 of the world's 9400 species occur in Australia and of those, about 300 can be found along the Shark Bay-Ningaloo coast and Outback Pathways. Every habitat has birds in it and in this book are only those that you will most likely see. Birds are great thermometers of the health of each system, a joy to observe and always a challenge to see clearly and be able to identify them and which breeding phase they are in.

Vagrants and migrants pass through at various times of the year. Any few minutes spent quietly watching and waiting will be well rewarded in this area. The JIZZ of a bird, from the US Air Force's GISS (General Indication of Shape and Size for enemy aircraft identification), is also a great way to identify each species. This takes practice but once learned will allow you to pick bird species much faster. The way it flies, wing shapes, swooping, diving and landing behaviour all add to this.

Bird nests and their shapes, size, location and what they are made of all add to determining which bird owns it. The creek banks, especially near water holes, will often have honeyeater nests that look like debris caught in the branches and sometimes you will see lots of similar nests in a small area of larger trees indicating more social species. Do not attempt to see the eggs or chicks as this can cause damage to the nest, frighten chicks out of the nest or send the adults away at the wrong time. Nesting sea birds on the islands will fly from their nests when approached by humans and the Silver Gulls have learned that this means free food in the form of unprotected chicks and eggs – so stay well away from them.

More than 30 species of seabirds have been recorded in the region. As this area is the overlap of southern and northern plant communities we see a similar overlap of bird species.

Migratory bird species, especially waders, feed along our coast during summer and return to the Northern Hemisphere to nest during our winter. Several species of native shorebirds like the Pied Oyster Catchers live, feed and breed on this coast and the herons, ibis and plovers or lapwings will be seen wherever there is open water.

Should you see any adult bird exhibiting distress or agitated behaviour it usually means they have a nest nearby – walk away until they return to normal as you may inadvertently tread on their eggs or chicks which are extremely well camouflaged in the nests.

male Crimson
at keeps an eye
t for lunch - an
ect.

LEN ZELL

Birdwatching

LEN ZELL

To maximise your pleasure in watching birds there are a few rules to follow:
· Find a guide book on Australian birds that works best for you.
  · Ask CALM for a species list for each area you go to and try to learn as many as possible before you come.
  · Know which species occur in each habitat before you get there.
· Ensure your binoculars work well for birds.
· Try not to disturb nesting birds – especially on seabird islands where gulls will then take the chicks and eggs.
· Share your sightings with those of less luck.
· Follow the directions of your guide.
· If you see a colour-coded leg band or wing tag on a dead or alive bird then record the information below (any photographs would be helpful) and contact the ABBBS with the following information;
- the band number
- where you found the band
- when you found the band (date)
- what you think happened to the bird
- where the bird is now
- where the band is now
- notes about any other marks on the bird.
If the bird is dead, we would like you, if possible, to;
- take the band off,
- gently straighten it as much as you can,
- stick it to some cardboard
- write the band number onto the cardboard
- write whether you have telephoned the ABBBS about this band
- send the band to the ABBBS
The ABBBS will be very glad to hear from you and will send you a letter telling you about where and when the bird was banded.
Send to:
The Australian Bird and Bat Banding Scheme (ABBBS)
GPO Box 8
CANBERRA ACT 2601
Telephone (02) 62742407 Facsimile (02) 62742455
Email: abbbs@deh.gov.au
or use On-line reporting: www.deh.gov.au/biodiversity/science/abbbs/recovery.html

N ZELL

Australian Bustard – stands to 1.5m, plains, grassland or open woodland dweller, now generally rare.

LEN ZELL

Emu - large flightless birds, males incubate eggs and tend young until independent, fruit and vegetable eaters.

N ZELL

Australian Pelicans fish cooperatively herding prey against obstacle or ring of birds.

LEN ZELL

Eastern Reef Herons - here the two colour morphs, harsh croaking call, feed on any exposed flats especially reefs.

N ZELL

Brahminy Kite - medium sized fish and carrion-eating raptore, common along coast.

LEN ZELL

White-breasted Brown Falcon - variable colour phases, upswept wings in flight, always dark thighs.

N ZELL

White-bellied Sea-Eagle – distinctive glide shape feeding on fish and sea snakes. Up to 80cm, builds enormous nests, lays two eggs.

www.osprey.com

Osprey – have large, conspicuous nests used for many years. These raptors feed on fish. 1.5m wingspan.

N ZELL

Little Stints - many wading birds come south to feed in Australia during our summer, then breed in Eurasia.

LEN ZELL

Pied Oystercatchers - very distinct colours and calls, usually in pairs, common on beaches and in estuaries.

BIRDS

LEN ZELL

Little Crows - stick cup nest with 3-6 eggs, carrion eater, social, acrobatic fliers.

LEN ZELL

Silver Gull on left and Paci **Gull** (western form) gregarious web-foote scavengers, 2-4 eggs.

LEN ZELL

Yellow-throated Minors - social, insect and nectar eaters, 3-4 eggs in untidy nest hung in leaves or fork.

LEN ZELL

Crimson Chat - females pla brown and white bell numbers increase after rai nest in loose colonies, 3 egg

LEN ZELL

Crested Pigeon - one of bronzewings, eats seeds, wings whistle in flight, cocks tail on ground often, messy twig nest.

LEN ZELL

Spinifex Pigeon - sma reddish bronzewing, i Spinifex or open grassland western form has red belly.

LEN ZELL

Corellas - western form - very social, noisy, eat seeds, 2-3 eggs in hollows, short white crest.

LEN ZELL

Singing Honeyeaters shrubland and woodlands, 2 3 eggs in flimsy nest in for on some islands, eats necta and insects.

PHIL DODD

Wedge-tailed Eagle – to 90cm height, high soaring eagle, enormous stick nests in trees, 1-3 eggs, carrion feeder.

LEN ZELL

Bush Thick-knee distinctive wailing calls night, 1-2 eggs, foun anywhere good leaf litter o ground, well camouflaged.

Mammals

These include the Bottlenose Dolphins, Humpbacked Whales and Dugong which are the primary drawcard species for most visitors to the coast. For all it is best that you use the directions of the CALM staff and ideally commercial operators to access the areas where they occur. All have specific behaviours and common locations and therefore the guides will maximise your chances of seeing the animals, ensure you behave properly so as not to distress them and also throw in a lot of great information adding to your enjoyment.

Sheep, goats, cattle, foxes and rabbits are the most commonly-seen mammals with kangaroos and Euros next. The use of a good spotlight on a moonless night will give you best mammal-spotting and for many other animals as well. Keep the spot as close to your eyes as possible so the reflection from the eye of the animal comes straight back to your eye. A few degrees off and you may miss it.

Dugong occur all along the coast and will surface, breathe, and be gone within seconds. You need to be patient, silent and still. If you are snorkelling in seagrass areas you can hear the 'crunch, crunch' sounds of them grazing. Their feeding trails appear as muddy clouds in the water and meandering bare tracks in the seagrass.

Humpback, Minke, Bryde's, Blue, Sperm and Killer Whales all occur off this coast. Humpbacks are the most commonly seen during their annual migration to the north for breeding during winter and then southwards to the Antarctic during spring to feed all over summer. The other species generally occur well offshore and are less commonly seen.

The Bottlenose Dolphins seen at Monkey Mia are the most common species. Others include Spinner, Indo-Pacific Humpbacked, Common, Spotted and Risso's Dolphins.

Southern Elephant Seals and Australian Sea Lions have been seen as rare visitors.

AMMALS

ISIE BEDFORD

Echidnas or Spiny Anteaters roll into a ball or burrow if caught in the open, eats ants and colonial insects, egg laying mammal.

LEN ZELL

Black-footed Rock-wallaby - agile rock hoppers, often seen basking in sun, rare.

Euro - Common Wallaroo - found throughout region, hard to distinguish from bigger Red Kangaroo.

N ZELL

Dugong - Sea Cows - grazing marine mammals, dense skeleton helps keep it down, broad tail allows fast swim if needed.

www.monkeymiawildsights.com.au

MAMMALS

Humpback Whales - to 15m and 45 tonnes, filter-feeding baleen whale, come north in winter to give birth and mate.

LEN ZELL

Dingo - beautifully-shaped dogs, usually solitary, introduced from SE Asia.

LEN ZELL

Bottlenose Dolphins – common worldwide, feed on fish, amazing sonar systems allow them to "see sound pictures" of surrounds and prey.

Important Contacts
and Agencies

Western Australia Department of Indigenous Affairs

All Aboriginal artefacts, painting and grave sites are fully protected by law.

Aboriginal Lands – Management and Policies can be obtained from the:

Aboriginal Affairs Department
PO Box 7770
Cloisters Square Perth WA 6000

If you want permits to visit sites and enter Aboriginal lands contact them or the Permits Officer on 08 9235 8000. As they have to contact the traditional owners before issuing a permit give them at least four-six weeks' notice. There are normally no problems getting a permit.

Or use the Easy Call Line - 1300 651 077. Dial this number from anywhere within Western Australia and you will automatically be connected to your regional DIA office for the cost of a local call.

Department of Indigenous Affairs
Ph (08) 9235 8000
Fax (08) 9235 8088
PO Box 7770,
Cloister's Square Perth WA 6850
Level 1, 197 St Georges Terrace Perth WA
Email info@dia.wa.gov.au
www.aad.wa.gov.au

Yamatji Land and Sea Council

(08) 9964 5645
Thoo Thoo Warninha Aboriginal Corporation - Cue
(08) 9963 1042
Yamaji Language Centre – works on the recording, retrieval, maintenance and promotion of the traditional languages and culture for the wider community.
32 Holland St
PO Box 433 Geraldton WA 6531
Ph (08) 9964 3550
Fax (08) 9964 4690
Burringurrah Community Aboriginal Corporation PMB 200
Meekatharra WA 6642
Ph (08) 9943 0967

Marine and National Parks

All native animals and plants in Western Australia are protected under the Wildlife Conservation Act. It is an offence for anyone to collect, interfere with or disturb wildlife or to gather, cut, remove or destroy plants unless they hold a permit from DEC.

There are many areas protected under various Acts and as they change with the progress of legislation it is best that you contact DEC or Fisheries (see below). Researchers believe that fish stocks are now at the limit of their harvesting capacity so please read the rules and follow the bag limits and size restrictions imposed.

Department of Environment and Conservation – DEC

168 St Georges Tce
Perth WA 6000
Tel: (08) 6467 5000
Fax (08) 6467 5562
www.dec.wa.gov.au

Postal Address
Locked Bag 104
Bentley Delivery Centre 6983

Regional Office
1st Floor, The Foreshore Centre
PO Box 72 Geraldton WA 6530
Ph (08) 9921 5955

District Offices
Knight Tce Denham WA 6537
Ph (08) 9948 1208
22 Nimitz St
PO Box 201 Exmouth WA 6707
Ph (08) 9947 1676

Local Office
211 Robinson St PO Box 500
Carnarvon WA 6701
Ph (08) 9941 3754
Fax (08) 9941 1801
Mobile 0427 413 754
Sat Phone 0405 182 708

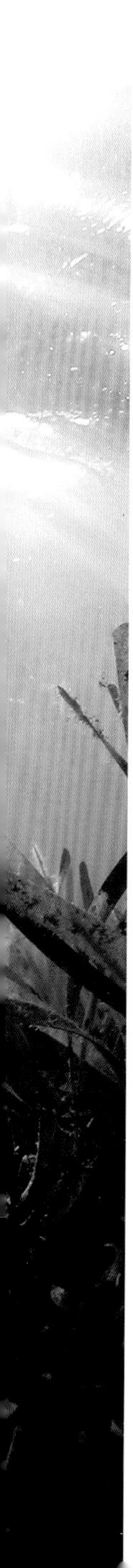

Department of Fisheries
Head Office
3rd Floor, The Atrium
168-170 St George's Terrace
Perth WA 6000

Locked Bag 39
Cloisters Square WA 6850
Ph (08) 9482 7333
Fax (08) 9482 7389
Fish Watch: 1800 815 507
www.fish.wa.gov.au/contact.html

Carnarvon Regional Office
59 Olivia Tce
PO Box 774 Carnarvon WA 6701
Ph (08) 9941 1185
Fax (08) 9941 1951

Denham District Office
Knight Terrace Denham WA 6537
Ph (08) 9948 1210
Fax (08) 9948 1154

Exmouth District Office
Cnr Riggs and Payne St
Exmouth WA 6707
Ph (08) 9949 2755
Fax (08) 9949 1558

Quarantine in WA
There are many fruits, vegetables and other items that carry diseases, weeds, insects and other things from one area to another. Check with the quarantine offices before moving from area to another as fines and the effects of transfer can be dramatic.

Agriculture Western Australia
WA Quarantine and Inspection Service
3 Barron-Hay Crt South Perth WA 6151
Ph (08) 9368 3333
Fax (08) 9474 2405
www.agric.wa.gov.au

Yacht Clubs
Carnarvon Yacht Club
2 West St (PO Box 369) Carnarvon WA 6701

hutchi@wn.com.au

Exmouth Yacht Club
Town Beach (PO Box 190) Exmouth WA 6707
Ph (08) 9949 1549
sail@exmouthyachtclub.org

Wastes at Sea
No human wastes can be dumped within 3m of any coast. No dumping of plastics in any form is allowed and all other rubbish should be taken ashore to be disposed of in local waste disposal systems.

Western Australian Museum
W.A Museum (Perth site)
Perth Cultural Centre
James St Perth WA 6000
Ph (08) 9212 3700
www.museum.wa.gov.au

WA Maritime Museum
Victoria Quay Fremantle WA 6160
Ph (08) 9431 8334

Tourism Western Australia
Level 9, 2 Mill St Perth WA 6000
GPO Box X2261 Perth WA 6847
Ph (08) 9262 1700
Fax (08) 9262 1702
www.westernaustralia.com

Tourism Midwest
PO Box 101 Geraldton WA 6531
Ph (08) 9921 3999
Fax (08) 9964 2445
info@tourismmidwest.com.au
www.tourismmidwest.com.au

Gascoyne Development Commission
Carnarvon (Head Office):
1st Floor 34 Stuart Street
Carnarvon WA 6701
Ph (08) 9941 7000
Fax (08) 9941 2576
Free Call: 1800 061 173
www.gdc.wa.gov.au

Exmouth:
Maidstone Crescent
Exmouth WA 6707
Ph (08) 9949
Fax (08) 9949 1618

Mid West Development Commission
Ground Floor, SGIO Bldg
45 Cathedral Ave PO Box 238
Geraldton WA 6531
Ph (08) 9921 0702
Fax (08) 9921 0707
www.mwdc.wa.gov.au

Weather
www.bom.gov.au/weather/wa

WA Coastal Marine Warnings
1300 659 223
WA Marine Service:
1900 926 150
Fax Information
1800 061 436

Local Shire Councils
Shire of Cue
2 Austin St, Cue WA 6640
Ph (08) 9963 1041
Fax (08) 9963 1085
cueshire@bigpond.com

Firearms
WA Police Service Firearms Branch
210 Adelaide Terrace Perth WA 6004
Ph (08) 9223 7000
Fax (08) 9223 7029
www.police.wa.gov.au/services/
FirearmsandWeapons.asp?

Maps
Hema Maps
25 McKechnie Drive (PO Box 4365)
Eight Mile Plains QLD 4113
Ph (07) 3340 0000
Fax (07) 3340 0099
manager@hemamaps.com.au
www.hemamaps.com.au

Department of Land Administration -
Mapping Section
1 Midland Square
Morrison Rd
PO Box 2222
Midland WA 6936
Ph (08) 9273 7373
Fax (08) 9273 7666
www.dola.wa.gov.au
mailroom@dli.wa.gov.au

Safety Guides
RoadWise – Free outback road safety
survival guide – call (08) 9213 2066

Some more Web Sites
www.australia.com/campaigns/
nationallandscapes/NingalooSharkBay.htm
www.DEC.wa.gov.au
www.sharkbay.org.au
www.steeppoint.com.au
www.exmouth-australia.com
www.fish.wa.gov.au
www.gdc.wa.gov.au
www.mainroads.wa.gov.au
www.outbackcoast.com.au
www.sharkbay.org
www.sharkbay.asn.au
www.sharkbay.wa.gov.au
www.ningaloo-atlas.org.au/
www.carnarvon.wa.gov.au
www.csiro.au/partnerships/Ningaloo-
Cluster.html#1

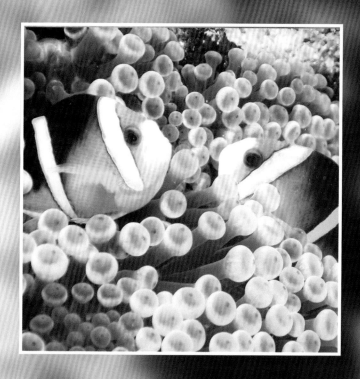

Books and Articles to Read

There are many historical and small family or local books available at each of the Information Centres and retailers in each town – seek them out – they are worth it!

The 5500-km-long boundary flow off western and southern Australia K. R. Ridgway and S. A. Condie J. Geophys. Res., 109, C04017, doi:10.1029/2003JC001921, 2004

World Heritage Area Nomination (WHAN) – Ningaloo Coast 2010

Understanding Aboriginal Culture – Cyril Havecker – 2002 – Cosmos Periodicals – ISBN 0 9588588 0 2

Yammatji – Aboriginal Memories of the Gascoyne- Bryan Clarke – 1992 – Hesperian Press – ISBN 0 85905 159 5

Archaeology of the Dreamtime: the story of prehistoric Australia and its people – Josephine Flood – Angus and Robertson – ISBN 0 2071 8448 8

The Jigalong Mob: Aboriginal Victors of the Desert Crusade – R Tonkinson – 1974 – Cummings Publishing Co Inc – ISBN 0 8465 7549 3

Jandamarra and the Bunuba Resistance – Howard Pedersen and Banjo Woorunmurra – 2000 – Magabala Books Aboriginal Corporation ISBN 1 875641 60 2

Aborigines of the West Their Past and Their Present – R M Berndt & C H Berndt Edits. – University of Western Australia Press – 1979 – ISBN 0 7301 0422 2

Wajarri Wisdom – Estelle Leyland – 2002 – Yamaji Language Centre – ISBN 1 875661 06 9

Redbill – From pearls to peace – the life and times of a remarkable lugger – Kate Lance – 2004 – Fremantle Arts Centre Press – ISBN 1 920731 42 3

Just a Century Ago – A History of the Shire of Cue – 1987 – PR Haydon (OAM) Hesperian Press ISBN 0 85905 110 2

The Future Eaters: An Ecological History of the Australian Land and People – Tim Flannery – Grove Press – 2002 – ISBN 0 8021 3943 4

Columbus Was Last – Patrick Huyghe – 1992 – MJF Books – ISBN 1-56731-577-1

What's in a Name? Place Names of the Gascoyne – 2004 – Paquita Boston – ISBN 0-9756744-0-4

The Challenge and the Chance – K Forrest – Hesperian Press Victoria Park WA – 1996 – ISBN 0 85905 217 6

Aboriginal Tribes of Australia – N B Tindale – 1984 – Australian National University Press – Canberra

1421 - The Year China Discovered the World – Gavin Menzies – Bantam Press, London

King of the Australian Coast – The Work of Phillip Parker King in the Mermaid and Bathurst 1817-1822 – Marsden Hordern – 1997 – ISBN 0 522 84720 X

Yalgoo – Alex Palmer – 1985 – Lap Industries – ISBN 0 9590584 0 0

Gascoyne Days – Jack Valli – 1983 – St George Books – ISBN 0 86778 019 3

The wreck of the barque Stefano off the North West Cape of Australia in 1875, 1999 – Gustave Rathe – Hesperian Press – ISBN 0 85905 144 7

Capes and Captains: a comprehensive study of the Australian coast – Rainer Radok, Surrey Beatty Publishers – 1990 – ISBN 0 9493 2428 0

WA Tide Tables – with best fishing times Including the Annual Boating Book – annual publication available at all newsagents, boating and fishing shops.

A Varied and Versatile Life the Memoirs of Frank Wittenoom 1855-1939 – RFB Lefroy – 2003 – Hesperian Press – ISBN 085905 317 2.

Australian Bush Survival Skills – Kevin Casey – 2000 – Kimberley Publications – ISBN 0 9587628 1 3

Shark Bay Through Four Centuries 1616 to 2000 – Hugh Edwards – 1999 – ISBN 0 957 75400 0

Shark Bay Legends – Russell Cooper – 1997 – L J Cogan Publisher – ISBN 0-9587406-0-7

Biodiversity of the southern Carnarvon Basin – Edits. A H Burbidge, M S Harvey & N L McKenzie – *Records of the Western Australian Museum* Supplement No 61 – ISBN 0 7307 5780 – ISSN 0 313 122X

Research in Shark Bay. Berry, P.F., Bradshaw, S.D. and Wilson, B.R. (Eds.). Report of the France-Australe Bicentenary Expedition Committee. Western Australia Museum – ISBN 0 7309 3919 7

Biogeography of Cape Range Western Australia – Edit. W F Humphreys – *Records of the Western Australian Museum* Supplement No 45, 1993 – ISSN 0313-122X – ISBN 0 7309 5947 3

Mangroves of Western Australia – V. Semeniuk, K. F. Kenneally & P. G. Wilson – Handbook No 12, Western Australia's Naturalist's Club 1978 ISBN 0 959 8452 3 2

Hazardous Animals of North-Western Australia – Carolyn Thomson, Barbara York Main and Kevin Crane – Dept of Conservation and Land Management – Bush Books – 1996 – ISBN 0 7309 7039 6

Indo-Pacific Coral Reef Guide – G R Allen & R Steene – 1994 – Tropical Reef Research – ISBN 981 00 5687 7

The Marine Fishes of Western Australia – G R Allen & Roger Swainston – Western Australian Museum – ISBN 0 7309 2113 1

Sea Snakes – Harold Heatwole – UNSW Press – 1999 – ISBN 0 868 40776 3

Reptiles and Amphibians of Australia – Harold G Cogger – 2000 – Reed – ISBN 1 876334 339

A Field Guide to Australian Birds – Graham Pizzey and Roy Doyle – Princeton University Press – 1987 – ISBN 0 6910 8483 1

Field Guide to the Birds of Australia – K. Simpson and N. Day – Viking O'Neill – 1999 Penguin – ISBN 0 670 87918 5

The Slater Field Guide to Australian Birds – Peter Slater, Pat Slater and Raoul Slater – 2002 – Reed New Holland – ISBN 876 334 71 1

A Field Guide to the Mammals of Australia – Peter Menkhorst & Frank Knight – Oxford University Press – 2001 – ISBN 0 19 550 870 X

Complete Book of Australian Mammals – Ronald Strahan – Editor Australian Museum – 1983 – ISBN 0 207 14454 0

Tracks, Scats and Other Traces – a Filed Guide to Australian Mammals – B Triggs – 2002 Oxford University Press – ISBN 0 19 5536436

North Australian Fish Finder – a magazine style advertising book published by The Editor's Office PO Box 3195 Darwin 0801. www.fishfinderbooks.com

Fishing the West – Ross Cusack & Mike Roennfeldt – 2003 – ISBN 0 90969 990 9

Dive and Snorkel sites in Western Australia – DEC – 2002 – ISBN 0 7309 6486 8

Western Australian Cruising – Steve Laws – Editor – Fremantle Sailing Club – 2001 – ISBN 0-9579804-0-7

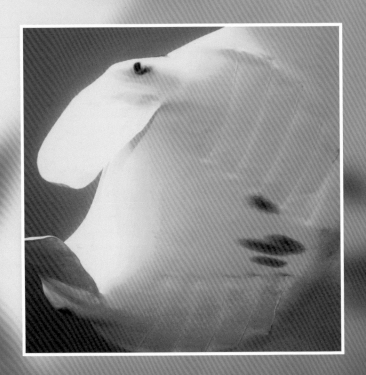

Index

MAPS LEGEND

Freeway / Divided Highway		Reef / Cay ; Shoal / Bank / Patch	
Major Highway		Swamp	
Major Road - sealed / unsealed		Subject to Inundation	
Minor Road - sealed / unsealed		Saline Coastal Flat	
Track - 4WD only		Mangrove	
Walking Track		Sand	
Proposed Road		Mountain / Hill	+ Mt Augustus
Road Distance (kilometres)	100 / 50	Sandridges	
National Highway Number		Cliffs	
National Route Number	96	Camping Area with facilities	
State Route Number		Bush Camping	
Tourist Route Number		Roadside Rest Area with water / toilet	
Golden Quest Discovery Trail	Q		
Kingsford Smith Mail Run		Roadside Rest Area with overnight camping	
Miners Pathway		Outback Rest Area (no facilities)	
Pioneers' Pathway			
Wool Wagon Pathway		Accommodation	
Warlu Way		Station Stay	
Railway with Siding or Station		Caravan Park	
Disused Railway		Walking Track	
Pipeline		Kayaking / Canoeing	
Major City	**PERTH**	Snorkelling / Diving	
City	● **Geraldton**	Wildflowers	
Major Town	● **Carnarvon**	Lookout	
Major Township	● **Leonora**	Information Centre; Accredited	
Minor Township	● **Cue**	Airport	
Locality	○ Ajana	Airfield/Airstrip	
Major Aboriginal Community	◉ **Burringurrah**	Unleaded & Diesel available 24 hours	24
Minor Aboriginal Community	✳ Kurrawang	Unleaded & Diesel (outback areas only)	
Homestead	• 'Tamala'	Autogas (outback areas only)	
Point of Interest	● Memorial	Hospital / Medical Facility (outback areas only)	
National Park			
Other Parks & Reserves		Police Station (outback areas only)	
State Forest / Timber Reserve			
Aboriginal Land		Royal Flying Doctor Service Base	
Native Title - Exclusive; Non Exclusive		Mine Site - Operating; Abandoned	
Scientific Reserve		**Insets Only**	
Prohibited Area; Heritage Site			
Marine Park		Picnic Area	
Permanent Lake		Ranger Station	
Mainly Dry Lake/Salt Lake		Drinking Water	
Waterhole / Rockhole / Pool	● Hamins Pool	Toilets; Toilets for Disabled	
Bore / Tank / Well	○ Well 3	Showers	
Shipwreck		BBQ / Fireplace	